FOREIGN INVESTMENTS
AND THE
NEW MIDDLE EAST:

A Survey of Prospects, Problems, and Planning Strategies

A. Kapoor

Professor of Marketing and International Business
New York University

with the assistance of Arthur Haast

THE DARWIN PRESS, INC.
PRINCETON, NEW JERSEY

The Darwin Press, Inc.
P. O. Box 2202
Princeton, N. J. 08540

Library of Congress Cataloging in Publication Data

Kapoor, Ashok, 1940-
    Foreign investments and the new Middle East.

    Bibliography: p.114
    1. Investments, Foreign--Near East. 2. Investments, Near East. 3. Business enterprises--Near
East. I. Haast, Arthur, joint author. II. Title.
HG5710.8.A3K35   332.6'73'0956   75-34650
ISBN 0-87850-027-8

Portions of Chapter Four are reprinted with permission, from PLANNING FOR INTERNATIONAL BUSINESS NEGOTIATIONS, by A. Kapoor, copyright 1975, Ballinger Publishing Company.

Printed in the United States of America

CONTENTS

CHARTS, GRAPHS, TABLES, AND FIGURES

4

FOREIGN INVESTMENTS AND THE NEW MIDDLE EAST

Prefatory Note and Acknowledgments

THE MIDDLE EAST has assumed new significance in international affairs; as a result, foreign companies are eager to develop the skills necessary for dealing successfully with Middle Eastern countries. Traditionally, U.S. companies outside of the petroleum and a few defense sectors have been largely ignorant of the Middle East because of a lack of economic potential in the region. The sudden and dramatic escalation of crude oil prices and the resultant short- and long-term surge of earnings of many Middle Eastern countries have created attractive new markets for the goods and services of companies from the U.S. and elsewhere.

The purpose of this study is to offer: 1) the views of executives of U.S. companies at the corporate level regarding the foreign investment climate in selected Middle Eastern countries (Iran, Egypt, and Saudi Arabia) at present (late 1974) and in five years (1979); 2) the attitudes, as perceived by U.S. corporate executives, of Middle Eastern oil-producing countries with surplus revenues toward investing in the United States and in developing countries of Asia; and 3) the role of the international company (hereafter referred to as IC) in such investments.

Chapter 1 offers an overview of the Middle East by highlighting the new economic resources of the region, the ambitious development

plans, and the increasing amounts of American investments and trade in the region.

Chapter 2 offers the views of the responding executives on the investment climate in Iran, Egypt, and Saudi Arabia, with reference to the following questions:

1. Existing operations: What types of operations are maintained in the Middle East at present?

2. Foreign investment objectives: What are the key objectives of American companies in Iran, Egypt, and Saudi Arabia at present and in five years?

3. Interest potential: What is the level of interest of American companies in Iran, Egypt, and Saudi Arabia at present and in five years?

4. Political stability: How stable are the governments of Iran, Egypt, and Saudi Arabia at present and in five years?

5. Operational problems: What major operating problems are faced by American companies in Iran, Egypt, and Saudi Arabia at present and in five years?

6. Foreign ownership: What is the attitude at present of the host governments toward foreign ownership, and in what manner and why is it likely to change in five years?

7. Foreign competition: What is the present extent of non-U.S. competition faced by American companies in these countries, what is it likely to be in five years, and what are the reasons for the competitive strength of non-U.S. companies?

8. Relative attractiveness: What are the proposed annual changes in investment levels by American companies in Iran, Egypt,

and Saudi Arabia over the next five years? What is the relative ranking of these countries in terms of additional investments?

Chapter 3 presents the views of the responding executives on foreign investments by Iran and other Arab oil-producing countries with surplus revenues with reference to the following issues:

1. What investment objectives do these countries have at present and in five years toward the U.S. and the developing countries of Asia?

2. In what ways might the American company assist such investments in the developing countries of Asia?

Chapter 4 presents an approach to planning for business development in the new Middle East and highlights major strategic planning considerations along with action programs for the IC.

Appendix A provides a number of important "do's and don'ts" of doing business in the Middle East. Appendix B lists the obvious but often overlooked characteristics of doing business in the Middle East. A Bibliography has been included at the end.

METHODOLOGY

The primary data presented in this study is based on the response of 26 companies to a questionnaire mailed in the Fall of 1974. The following is an annual (1973) sales volume profile of these companies. Fifteen additional companies responded that they did not intend any significant involvement in the Middle East.

Sales	Number of Respondents	%
Less than $200 million	2	7.7
$200-$600 million	5	19.2
$601-$1,000 million	6	23.1
over $1,000 million	10	38.5
Other-Banks	3	11.5
Total	26	100.0

The largest response category is of companies over $1 billion in sales volume. The responding companies (presented below by Standard International Trade Classifications--SITC) are generally representative of American companies doing business in the Middle East when their services and trade products are compared with 1973 U.S. exports to the Middle East.

Group	Number* of Respondents	%	% of U.S. Exports
Food and Live Animals	3	10.0	13.9
Beverages and Tobacco	0	0	2.0
Crude Materials, Inedible, except Fuels	2	6.7	3.7
Minerals Fuels, Lubricants, and Related Materials	0	0	0.5
Animals and Vegetable Oils and Fats	0	0	2.6
Chemicals	5	16.7	4.3
Machinery and Transport Equipment	6	20.0	38.9
Manufactured Goods Classified by Materials	3	10.0	
Miscellaneous Manufactured Articles	3	10.0	9.2
Commodities and Transactions not classified according to kind including Military Equipment and Services	8	26.6	24.8
Total	30*	100.0	99.9

* A respondent might belong to more than one SITC.

The cooperation of many government officials and corporate executives is gratefully acknowledged.

October, 1975
New York City

A. Kapoor
Arthur Haast

1

OVERVIEW OF THE MIDDLE EAST

THE QUESTION explored in this chapter is: Why is the Middle East important to the IC from an economic standpoint?

ECONOMIC SIGNIFICANCE

Charts 1 and 2 present the relative role of the Middle East in world oil production and world proven oil reserves as of 1974. The importance of the Middle East as a source of crude oil will not diminish in the coming decade.

With the dramatic increase of crude oil prices, the five major oil-producing countries of the Middle East achieved an estimated $72.4 billion in revenues in 1974. The estimated individual country break-down is: Saudi Arabia, $28.9 billions; Iran, $20.9 billions; Kuwait, $8.5 billions; Iraq, $7.6 billions; United Arab Emirates, $6.5 billions.

The accumulation of wealth by the oil-producing countries is not, however, a short-term phenomenon. Table 1 offers a projection of the growth of oil revenues and surplus for the major Middle East oil-producing countries on a cumulative basis between 1973-1983.

Such an accumulation of economic resources presents, of course, exciting opportunities for trade and investments in the Middle East,

as well as investments by some Middle Eastern countries in other parts of the world. The needs and resources of the region require a long-range perspective by the IC in penetrating and developing Middle East markets.

TABLE 1

CUMULATIVE SURPLUSES, 1973-1983
($ billion)

	Estimated oil earnings	Estimated imports		Surplus	
		min.	max.	min.	max.
Saudi Arabia	177.6	53.3	88.8	88.8	124.3
Iran	175.9	140.7	175.9	0.0	35.2
Kuwait	72.0	28.8	43.2	28.8	43.2
Libya	69.2	34.6	41.5	27.7	34.6
Iraq	47.4	23.7	30.8	16.6	23.7
Algeria	34.0	30.6	34.0	0.0	3.4
Abu Dhabi	32.8	13.1	19.7	13.1	19.7
Qatar	14.3	5.7	8.6	5.7	8.6
Dubai	5.9	2.4	3.6	2.4	3.6
Oman	5.3	1.6	2.7	2.7	3.7
Total	634.5	334.5	448.7	185.8	300.0

Source: Mahdi al-Bazzaz, "Middle East Oil Revenues: An Assessment of their size and uses," *Middle East Economic Digest*, March 15, 1974.

The development plans, especially of the oil-producing countries, are ambitious. For example, Iran's plans will exhaust all of her oil-related earnings. Table 1 provides a broad range of the huge amounts the country is expected to spend on imports. Total fixed investments under the revised Fifth Development Plan (1973-1978) are $68.6 billions, as follows: oil and gas, 51.5%; industries and mines, 18%; services, 16.4%; and agriculture,

CHART 1   WORLD OIL PRODUCTION, 1974
(total: 56.7 million bpd)

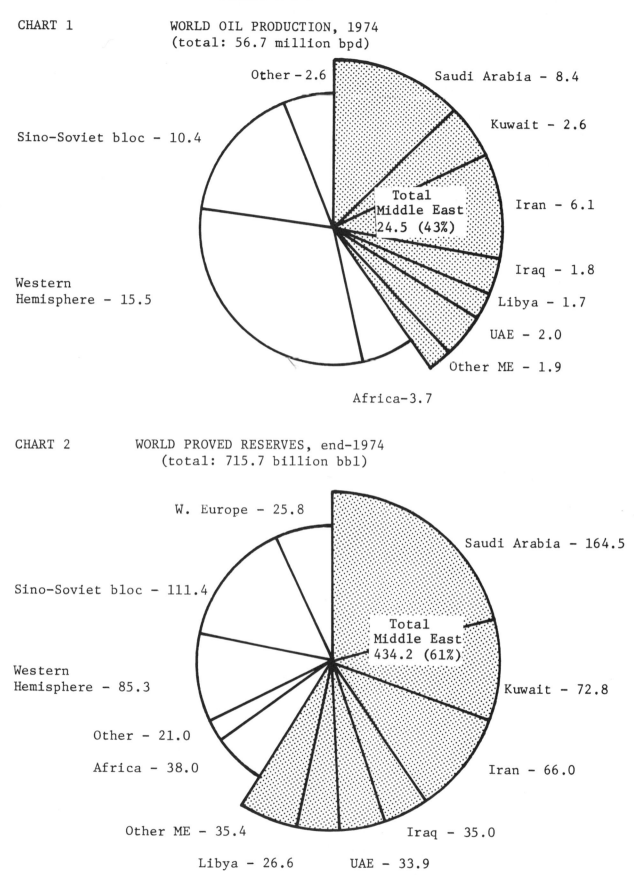

Other – 2.6

Saudi Arabia – 8.4

Kuwait – 2.6

Sino-Soviet bloc – 10.4

Total
Middle East
24.5 (43%)

Iran – 6.1

Iraq – 1.8

Libya – 1.7

Western
Hemisphere – 15.5

UAE – 2.0

Other ME – 1.9

Africa-3.7

CHART 2   WORLD PROVED RESERVES, end-1974
(total: 715.7 billion bbl)

W. Europe – 25.8

Saudi Arabia – 164.5

Sino-Soviet bloc – 111.4

Total
Middle East
434.2 (61%)

Western
Hemisphere – 85.3

Kuwait – 72.8

Other – 21.0

Iran – 66.0

Africa – 38.0

Other ME – 35.4

Iraq – 35.0

Libya – 26.6   UAE – 33.9

Source: Oil & Gas Journal

14

7%. U.S. exports and investments are increasing rapidly as are those of non-U.S. companies.

Egypt's development plans call for major investments in iron and steel, transport, communications, housing, energy, and agriculture industries. To attract foreign investment, including Arab surplus oil revenues, Egypt in 1974 passed a new foreign investment law permitting foreign ownership of business in Egypt, established a parallel foreign exchange market, and reactivated with the U.S. in July 1974 the United States Investment Guarantee Agreement which gives the Overseas Private Investment Corporation credits available for currency convertibility and insurance against expropriation and war risks. Loans and grants from Western and Arab oil-producing countries are likely to be a significant source of foreign exchange for Egypt. Other sources of foreign exchange will include exploration and development of Egypt's own oil reserves (petroleum companies currently have outstanding obligations of several hundred million dollars for oil exploration), opening of the Suez Canal, tourism, and exports of agriculture products (primarily cotton). However, Egypt faces severe foreign exchange limitations which directly influence the scope and pace of her development programs.

Saudi Arabia is rich from oil earnings and the nation has embarked on an ambitious development program. Estimated imports between 1973-1983 are between $53 billions-$88 billions. The second five year plan beginning in July 1975 has projected expenditures of over $140 billions to include infrastructure development in transportation, tele-communications, electrification, industrial diversification, water desalination, petroleum-related industries, and steel and aluminum.

Saudi Arabia is expected to loan, donate, and invest her oil revenue surpluses in other Arab countries, in the developing countries, and in the developed countries (notably the U.S.).

The challenge faced by the IC is to determine policies and programs on how to participate in a meaningful and lasting manner in assisting the host countries to achieve their objectives.

AMERICAN INVESTMENTS AND TRADE

Tables 2 and 3 present data on the amount of U.S. investment on an annual basis between 1968-1973, and the distribution of such investment between 1968-1973. Table 2 clearly shows that historically the Middle East has accounted for the smallest percentage of U.S. foreign direct investment of any developing region. However, the growing significance of the region is reflected in the 35% growth of foreign direct investment between 1972 and 1973 representing the largest percentage growth of any developing region. The post-1973 growth rate is of a very high magnitude. Nevertheless, the absolute amount of investment remains small.

Table 3 shows that petroleum has accounted for the lion's share of the investment followed by mining and smelting. Manufacturing and **service** sector investments have been minimal; yet, these are precisely the sectors in which major new investment opportunities are emerging as host countries seek to diversify their industrial base beyond petroleum.

Through 1972 U.S. trade with the Middle East was not important in relation to total world trade. The Middle East accounted for only 2.97% of total U.S. exports and 1.39% of imports in that year. Tables

T A B L E 2

U.S. PRIVATE INVESTMENTS OVERSEAS (1)

1968--1973

(In Millions of Dollars)

		1968	1969	1970	1971	1972	1973
Middle East (2)	$	1,805	1,805	1,617	1,661	1,992	2,682
	%	2.78	2.54	2.07	1.93	2.11	2.50
Africa (3)	$	1,978	2,227	2,614	2,871	3,091	2,830
	%	3.04	3.14	3.34	3.33	3.28	2.64
Latin America	$	13,101	13,858	14,760	15,789	16,798	18,452
	%	20.16	19.51	18.88	18.32	17.80	17.20
Far East	$	1,869	2,172	2,457	3,036	3,354	3,903
	%	2.88	3.06	3.14	3.52	3.56	3.64
Total Developing Countries	$	18,753	20,062	21,448	23,358	25,235	27,867
	%	28.86	28.25	27.43	27.10	26.75	25.98
Developed Countries	$	43,500	47,886	53,145	58,571	64,359	74,084
	%	66.94	67.41	67.98	67.95	68.22	69.06
Unallocated	$	2,731	3,085	3,586	4,270	4,743	5,317
	%	4.20	4.23	4.59	4.95	5.03	4.96
Total All Countries	$	64,983	71,033	78,178	86,198	94,337	107,268
	%	100.00	100.00	100.00	100.00	100.00	100.00

Source: Survey of Current Business, U.S. Department of Commerce, Investment figures are from issues of the survey between 1970 and 1974.

(1) Investments refer to book value and does not include portfolio
investment.

(2) Includes Bahrain, Iran, Iraq, Israel, Jordan, Kuwait, Lebanon,
Qatar, Saudi Arabia, Southern Yemen, Syria, Trucial States, Oman,
and Yemen.

(3) Includes Egypt and all other countries in Africa except South Africa.

Note: Columns may not add because of rounding.

17

T A B L E 3

DISTRIBUTION OF U.S. INVESTMENTS IN THE MIDDLE EAST

1968 - 1973

(In Millions of Dollars)

		Mining & Smelting	Petroleum	Manufacturing	Other Industries	Total
1968	$	3	1,656	63	83	1,805
	%	0.17	91.74	3.49	4.60	100.00
1969	$	3	1,627	80	95	1,805
	%	0.17	90.14	4.43	5.26	100.00
1970	$	3	1,442	85	87	1,617
	%	0.18	89.18	5.26	5.38	100.00
1971	$	3	1,464	92	102	1,661
	%	0.18	88.14	5.54	6.14	100.00
1972	$	5	1,767	104	116	1,992
	%	0.25	88.71	5.22	5.82	100.00
1973	$	5	2,377	130	170	2,682
	%	0.18	88.63	4.85	6.34	100.00

Source: Same as Table 2

T A B L E 4

U.S. EXPORTS OF PRINCIPAL COMMODITIES TO MAJOR WORLD AREAS

1968 - 1973

(In Million of Dollars)

		1968	1969	1970	1971	1972	1973
Middle East	$	1,094	1,344	1,423	1,816	1,974	3,041
	%	3.16	3.54	3.29	4.12	2.97	4.26
Africa	$	765	819	940	1,009	898	1,335
	%	2.21	2.15	2.17	2.29	1.80	1.87
Latin America	$	5,339	5,576	6,532	6,485	7,275	9,930
	%	15.41	14.67	15.11	14.70	14.61	13.92
Far East	$	3,582	3,495	4,029	4,047	4,373	6,609
	%	10.34	9.20	9.32	9.17	8.79	9.27
Total Developing Countries (1)	$	10,821	11,277	12,993	13,411	14,576	20,973
	%	31.24	29.67	30.06	30.39	29.28	29.41
Developed Countries	$	23,600	26,479	29,877	30,335	34,319	47,177
	%	68.14	69.67	69.12	68.74	68.94	66.15
Communist Areas	$	215	249	354	384	883	2,486
	%	0.62	0.66	0.82	0.87	1.77	3.49
Total Exports	$	34,636	38,006	43,224	44,130	49,778	71,314
	%	100.00	100.00	100.00	100.00	100.00	100.00

(1) Total includes exports to New Guinea and other islands of the Pacific.

Source: "Overseas Business Reports," U.S. Department of Commerce, June 1974, OBR 74-22.

Note: Columns may not add because of rounding.

U.S. EXPORTS OF PRINCIPAL COMMODITIES

TO THE MIDDLE EAST

1968 - 1973

(In Millions of Dollars)

		1968	1969	1970	1971	1972	1973
Food and Live Animals	$	124	110	143	183	202	422
	%	11.33	8.15	10.05	10.05	10.23	13.88
Beverages & Tobacco	$	21	26	28	36	45	61
	%	1.92	1.93	1.97	1.98	2.28	2.01
Crude Materials, Inedible Other Than Fuel	$	41	38	39	60	68	113
	%	3.75	2.83	2.74	3.30	3.44	3.72
Minerals, Fuels and Related Materials	$	7	7	8	8	13	14
	%	0.64	0.52	0.56	0.44	0.66	0.46
Animal and Vegetable Oils and Fats	$	16	29	54	67	65	80
	%	1.46	2.16	3.79	3.69	3.29	2.63
Chemicals	$	71	62	68	78	86	131
	%	6.49	4.61	4.78	4.30	4.36	4.31
Machinery & Transport Equipment	$	522	556	544	726	854	1,184
	%	47.71	41.37	38.23	38.98	43.26	38.93
Other Manufactured Goods	$	129	142	145	158	203	280
	%	11.79	10.57	10.19	8.70	10.28	9.21
Other Transactions	$	8	10	16	23	26	34
	%	0.73	0.74	1.12	1.27	1.32	1.12
Foreign (re-exports)	$	27	32	27	33	52	85
	%	2.47	2.38	1.90	1.82	2.63	2.80
"Special Category"	$	126	333	352	445	362	636
	%	11.52	24.78	24.74	24.50	18.34	20.91
Total	$	1.094	1,344	1,423	1,816	1,974	3,041
	%	100.00	100.00	100.00	100.00	100.00	100.00

Source: Same as Table 4

Note: Columns may not add because of rounding.

T A B L E   6

U.S. IMPORTS OF PRINCIPAL COMMODITIES FROM MAJOR WORLD AREAS

1968 - 1973

(In Millions of Dollars)

		1968	1969	1970	1971	1972	1973
Middle East	$	388	383	371	593	773	1,371
	%	1.17	1.06	0.93	1.30	1.39	1.98
Africa	$	834	762	800	931	1,254	2,178
	%	2.51	2.11	2.00	2.04	2.26	3.15
Latin America	$	5,143	5,163	5,836	6,038	7,004	9,559
	%	15.48	14.32	14.61	13.25	12.60	13.83
Far East	$	2,499	3,039	3,397	3,941	5,264	6,979
	%	7.52	8.43	8.50	8.65	9.47	10.10
Total Developing Countries (1)	$	8,886	9,373	10,442	11,549	14,356	20,169
	%	26.74	26.01	26.14	25.35	25.83	29.18
Developed Countries	$	24,130	26,460	29,259	33,744	40,822	48,327
	%	72.62	73.41	73.24	74.06	73.44	69.92
Communist Areas	$	200	198	227	229	354	585
	%	0.60	0.55	0.67	0.50	0.64	0.85
Total Imports	$	33,226	36,043	39,952	45,563	55,583	69,121
	%	100.00	100.00	100.00	100.00	100.00	100.00

(1) Total includes imports from New Guinea and other islands of the Pacific.

Source: Same as Table 4

Note: Columns may not add because of rounding.

T A B L E   7

U.S. IMPORTS OF PRINCIPAL COMMODITIES

FROM THE MIDDLE EAST

1968 - 1973

(In Millions of Dollars)

		1968	1969	1970	1971	1972	1973
Food and Live Animals	$	29	31	29	29	31	49
	%	7.47	8.09	7.82	4.89	4.01	3.57
Beverages & Tobacco	$	3	4	5	4	8	12
	%	0.77	1.04	1.35	0.67	1.03	0.88
Crude Materials, Ined-ible Other Than Fuels	$	35	26	28	30	42	47
	%	9.02	6.79	7.55	5.06	5.43	3.43
Minerals, Fuels and Related Materials	$	181	171	139	332	430	945
	%	46.65	44.65	37.47	55.99	55.63	68.93
Animal and Vegetable Oils and Fats	$	-	-	-	-	-	-
	%	-	-	-	-	-	-
Chemicals	$	3	3	5	7	12	14
	%	0.77	0.78	1.35	1.18	1.55	1.02
Machinery and Trans-port Equipment	$	2	4	8	6	9	18
	%	0.52	1.04	2.16	1.01	1.16	1.31
Other Manufactured Goods	$	121	134	137	163	215	263
	%	31.19	34.99	36.93	27.49	27.81	19.18
Other Transactions	$	14	10	19	23	27	23
	%	3.61	2.61	5.12	3.88	3.49	1.68
Total	$	388	383	371	593	773	1,371
	%	100.00	100.00	100.00	100.00	100.00	100.00

Source: Same as Table 4

Note: Columns may not add because of rounding.

4 and 6 illustrate U.S. exports and imports to major world areas, and

Tables 5 and 7 list the principal commodities exported to, and imported

from, the Middle East for the years 1968 to 1973. The year 1973, how-

ever, saw dramatic increases in both exports and imports.

U.S. exports to the Middle East in 1973 amounted to $3.041

million, an increase of 54% from 1972. The major export categories

in 1973, and those having the greatest increases from 1972 levels,

were machinery and equipment, special category (military equipment),

and food and live animals.

	Amount Exported in 1973	Increase from 1972 $	%
Machinery & Transport Equipment	$1,184 million	$330 million	39%
Special Category	636 million	274 million	76%
Food & Live Animals	422 million	220 million	109%

U.S. imports from the Middle East in 1973 increased 77% over

1972, to $1,371 million. Minerals, fuels, and related materials in

1973 accounted for 69% of total U.S. imports, an increase of $515

million or 120% from 1972. Imports of other manufactured goods,

primarily gem diamonds, was a distant second with $263 million.

2

Foreign Investment Climate in the Middle East

THIS SECTION presents views of U.S. executives on selected aspects
of the foreign investment climate in Iran, Egypt, and Saudi Arabia
at present (1974) and in five years (1979). Section 1 presents the
existing types of operations, objectives, and interest of companies;
Section 2 highlights important characteristics of the foreign investment climate; and Section 3 outlines the proposed plans for additional
investments. Policy implications and action programs in planning for
business development in the new Middle East are discussed in Chapter 4.

SECTION 1: OPERATIONS, OBJECTIVES, INTEREST

<u>Types of Operations at Present.</u> What types of operations are maintained
by the responding companies in the Middle East? The response to this
question indicates the existing orientation and base from which companies will escalate their involvement in the Middle East.

Graph 1 shows that by far the largest response category for Iran
is distributor/representative followed closely by sales office. Manufacturing for the host-country market is noted by a significant minority
of respondents especially when the "other" category is included in this
response. Pure sale of technology and services is noted by a small
percentage of respondents but this category is also likely to be

expressed in some of the other responses, notably under local manufacturing. A significant percentage (23%) of the respondents maintained no operations in Iran at the time of their response.

None of the companies intended to use Iran as a manufacturing base largely for exports. Over time, in light of Iran's desire to diversify its export base, foreign investors will face growing pressures from the host government for exports.

For the last two decades, Egypt has severely restricted the role of private companies (both domestic and foreign) in local operations, which explains the almost total absence of manufacturing operations in Egypt by the responding companies. Low-level commitments through distributor/representatives and sales office account for the vast majority of existing operations. A significant percentage (39%) of the responding companies do not maintain any operations in Egypt.

Very few companies maintain local manufacturing operations in Saudi Arabia. By far the largest single category of operations for U.S. companies is distributor/representative. A significant percentage (27%) of the responding companies did not have any operations in Saudi Arabia.

As the level of commitment to a country grows, a company increases allocation of resources and acceptance of a higher degree of risk. For example, in Egypt and Saudi Arabia, the operations of American companies at the time of response were of low commitment. For Iran, the U.S. company is characterized by a comparatively higher level of commitment.

GRAPH 1

DISTRIBUTION OF RESPONDING COMPANIES' TYPES OF
OPERATIONS IN THE MIDDLE EAST

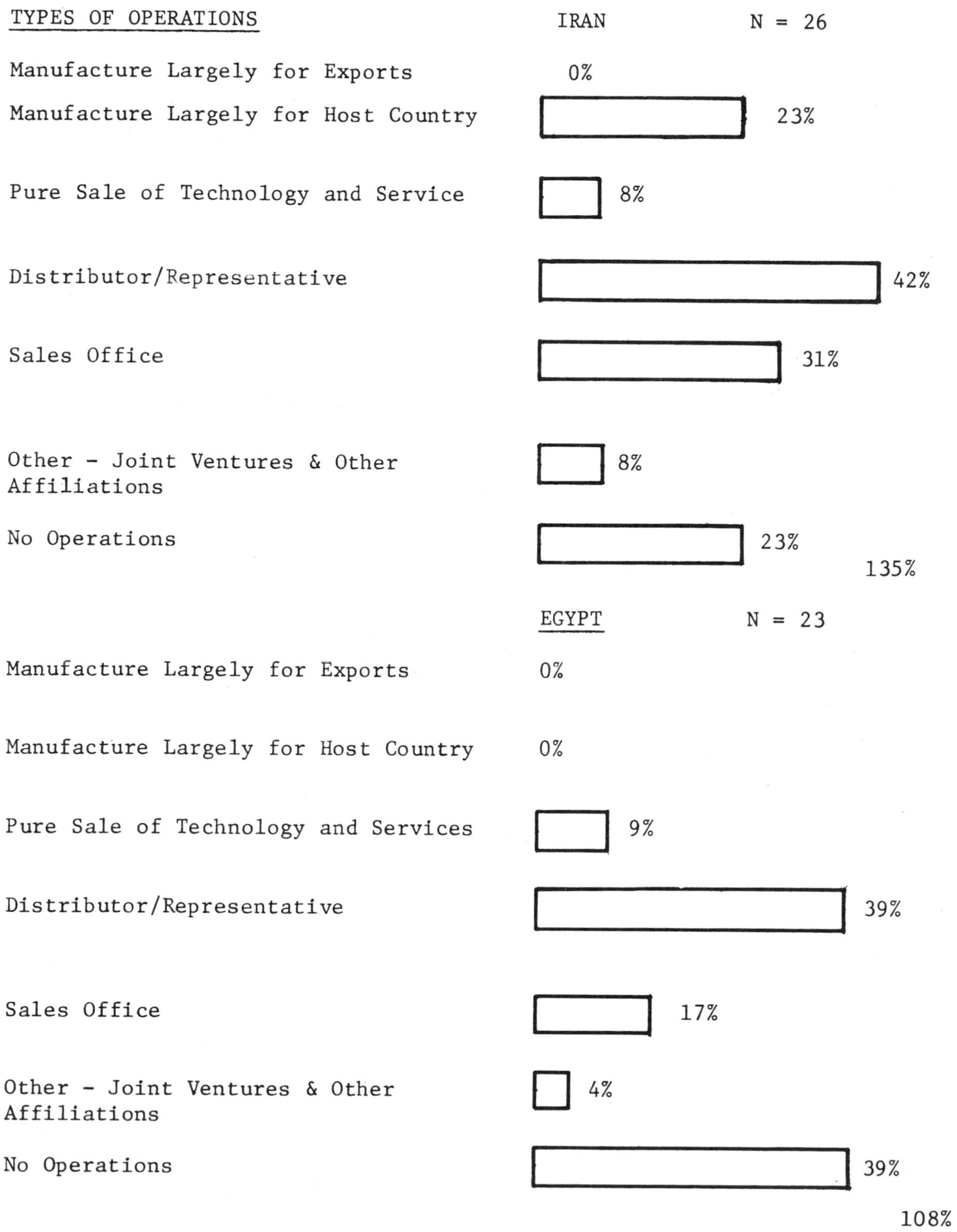

TYPES OF OPERATIONS	IRAN	N = 26
Manufacture Largely for Exports	0%	
Manufacture Largely for Host Country		23%
Pure Sale of Technology and Service		8%
Distributor/Representative		42%
Sales Office		31%
Other – Joint Ventures & Other Affiliations		8%
No Operations		23%
		135%

	EGYPT	N = 23
Manufacture Largely for Exports	0%	
Manufacture Largely for Host Country	0%	
Pure Sale of Technology and Services		9%
Distributor/Representative		39%
Sales Office		17%
Other – Joint Ventures & Other Affiliations		4%
No Operations		39%
		108%

Total by country exceeds 100% because some respondents have
more than one type of operation in the country.

26

GRAPH 1 (continued)

DISTRIBUTION OF RESPONDING COMPANIES' TYPES OF
OPERATIONS IN THE MIDDLE EAST

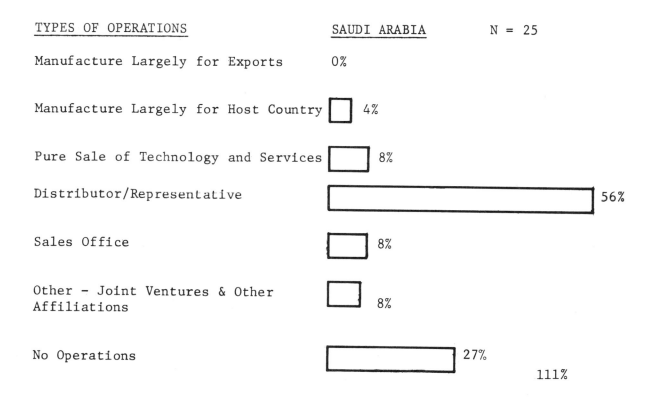

TYPES OF OPERATIONS   SAUDI ARABIA   N = 25

Manufacture Largely for Exports   0%

Manufacture Largely for Host Country   [ ] 4%

Pure Sale of Technology and Services   [ ] 8%

Distributor/Representative   [   ] 56%

Sales Office   [ ] 8%

Other - Joint Ventures & Other   [ ] 8%
Affiliations

No Operations   [   ] 27%
                                                 111%

Key Objectives. What are the objectives of the American company in
the Middle East at present and in five years (Graph 2)? The objectives will indicate the types of resources allocations which will be
required of U.S. companies for effective and continuous operations
in the Middle East.

By far the most important objective in Iran at present and in
five years is to develop Iran as a new export market for goods and
services. Local manufacturing to cater to host-country needs remains
the second most frequently stated objective. Pure sale of technology
and meeting moves of competitors are ranked in third and fourth place.
The major change in five years is the growth of manufacturing in
Iran largely for exports and efforts to keep up with moves of competitors.

The overall pattern of response for Egypt is not different from
Iran. Developing Egypt as a new export market is the primary objective at present and in five years. Local manufacturing and meeting
competitive moves gain in importance over time. As with Iran, local
manufacturing largely for exports shows a significant increase in
five years.

In general, the objectives of U.S. companies in penetrating Saudi
Arabia are similar to the response for Egypt and Iran. Developing new
export markets is the key objective. Local manufacturing at present
for the host country has far lower priority. The lowest priority at
present and in five years is attached to local manufacturing largely
for export.

Level of Interest. The level of interest of responding companies in

GRAPH 2

KEY OBJECTIVES OF U.S. COMPANIES IN SELECTED
MIDDLE EASTERN COUNTRIES - 1974 AND 1979

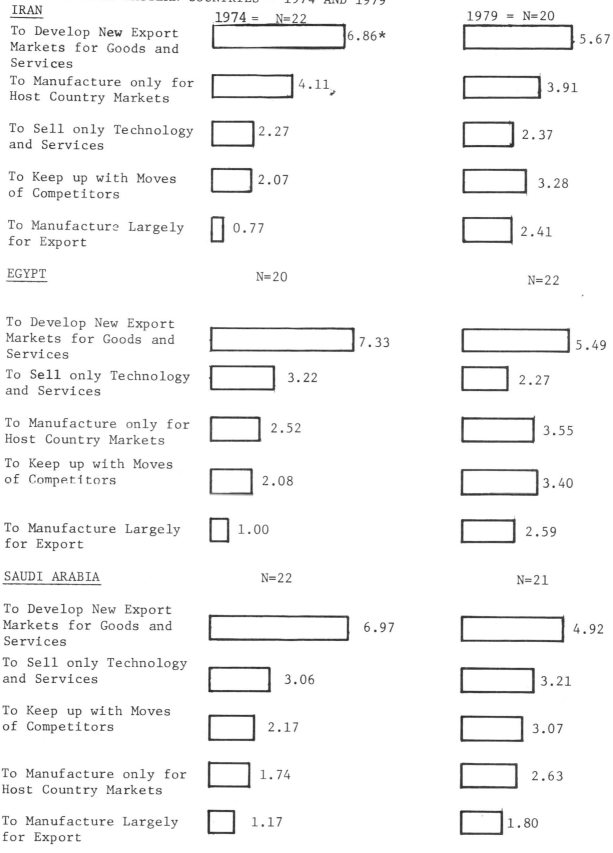

IRAN

1974 = N=22   1979 = N=20

To Develop New Export Markets for Goods and Services — 6.86* / 5.67

To Manufacture only for Host Country Markets — 4.11 / 3.91

To Sell only Technology and Services — 2.27 / 2.37

To Keep up with Moves of Competitors — 2.07 / 3.28

To Manufacture Largely for Export — 0.77 / 2.41

EGYPT   N=20   N=22

To Develop New Export Markets for Goods and Services — 7.33 / 5.49

To Sell only Technology and Services — 3.22 / 2.27

To Manufacture only for Host Country Markets — 2.52 / 3.55

To Keep up with Moves of Competitors — 2.08 / 3.40

To Manufacture Largely for Export — 1.00 / 2.59

SAUDI ARABIA   N=22   N=21

To Develop New Export Markets for Goods and Services — 6.97 / 4.92

To Sell only Technology and Services — 3.06 / 3.21

To Keep up with Moves of Competitors — 2.17 / 3.07

To Manufacture only for Host Country Markets — 1.74 / 2.63

To Manufacture Largely for Export — 1.17 / 1.80

*MAXIMUM VALUE = 10 if it is viewed as <u>the most important</u> by <u>all</u>
the respondents to the particular question.

Iran, Egypt, and Saudi Arabia at present and in five years is presented in Graph 3. The vast majority of responding companies are strongly interested in Iran both at present and in five years. The response patterns for Egypt and Saudi Arabia reveal observable differences from Iran.

For Egypt, the category reflecting the largest response is of "strong interest" followed by "limited interest." However, in five years, companies reveal a distinct growth of interest in Egypt with the largest response category being "very strong interest."

For Saudi Arabia, the two largest response categories are of "very strong interest" and "limited interest." In five years, there is an increase of interest in the "strong" and "very strong" categories but a significant minority continue to demonstrate "no" and "limited" interest.

What are the primary reasons for the level of interest at present and in 1979 (see Graphs 4, 5, 6). The choice of response falls into two broad categories--those conducive to a greater interest and those generally unfavorable. Considerable demand, an attractive investment climate, a potentially large domestic market, encouragement by the U.S. Government, and gaining access to host-country funds are examples of the former; political uncertainties, small market size, and more profitable opportunities elsewhere would tend to discourage interest in these countries.

Graph 4 indicates that the *potentially* large demand of the Iranian market is by far the main reason for interest of U.S. companies at present and in five years. The second most frequently stated reason is "considerable demand *at present*," followed by the creation of an

GRAPH 3

LEVEL OF INTEREST OF RESPONDING COMPANIES
IN SELECTED MIDDLE EASTERN COUNTRIES – 1974 AND 1979

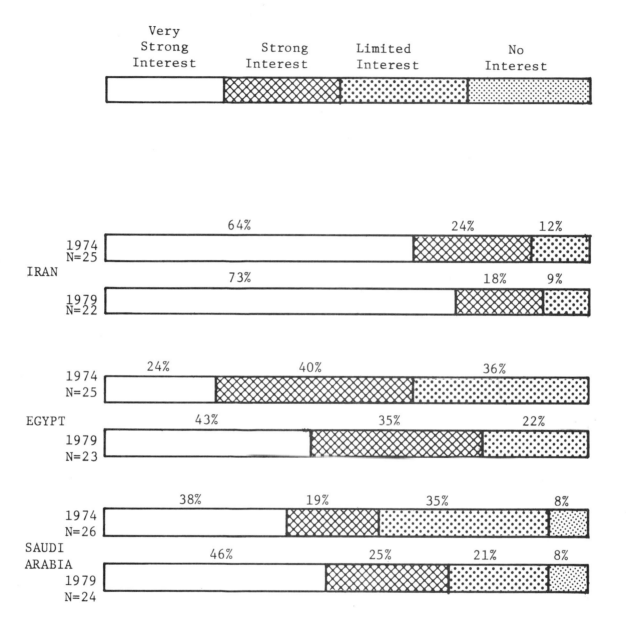

GRAPH 4

MAIN REASONS FOR LEVEL OF INTEREST
IN IRAN - 1974 AND 1979

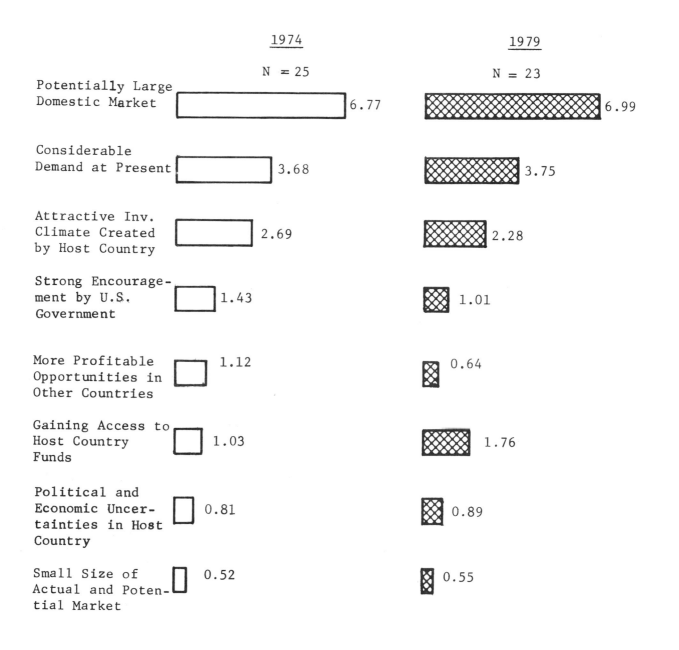

attractive investment climate by the host country. An observable shift
in five years is reflected in the response to "gaining access to host
country funds" which might be used in collaborative ventures in third
countries.

By far the dominating reason for interest in Egypt is the potentially large host-country market (Graph 5). The other considerations
are of far lesser importance for the responding companies. Unlike
Iran, Egypt is not considered to present significant current demand
and the ability to pay for it.

While the potentially large domestic market is the single most
important reason for interest in Saudi Arabia at present, other reasons
are close seconds (Graph 6). However, host-country demand becomes the
predominant reason in five years. As with Iran, the considerable
demand at present and the ability to pay for foreign goods and services is the second most important reason. A noticeable change is
reflected in five years in the response category of gaining access
to host country funds for possible use in third country collaborative
ventures.

SECTION 2: IMPORTANT CHARACTERISTICS

The investment climate of a country is composed of several dimensions.
The dimensions highlighted here are: stability of host governments,
extent of foreign ownership, major operating problems, extent of
foreign competition, and extent of future investment.

Stability of Host Governments. The degree of host-government stability
at present and in five years, as perceived by the responding companies,

33

GRAPH 5

MAIN REASONS FOR LEVEL OF INTEREST
IN EGYPT-1974 AND 1979

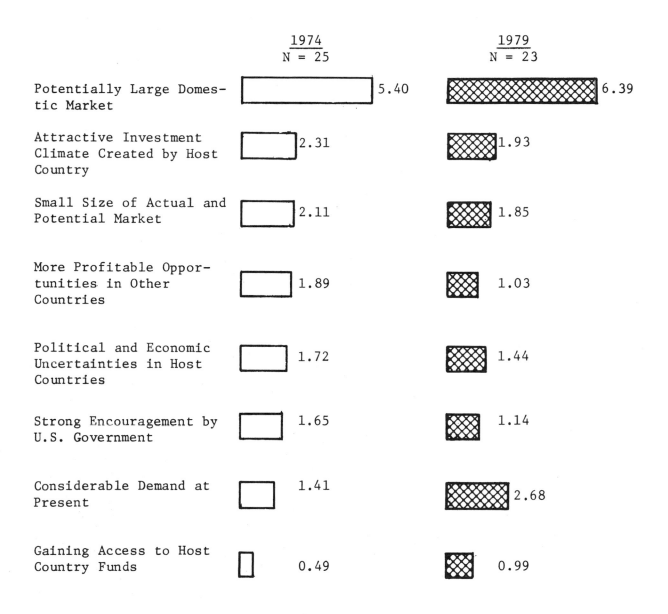

GRAPH 6

MAIN REASONS FOR LEVEL OF INTEREST
IN SAUDI ARABIA - 1974 AND 1979

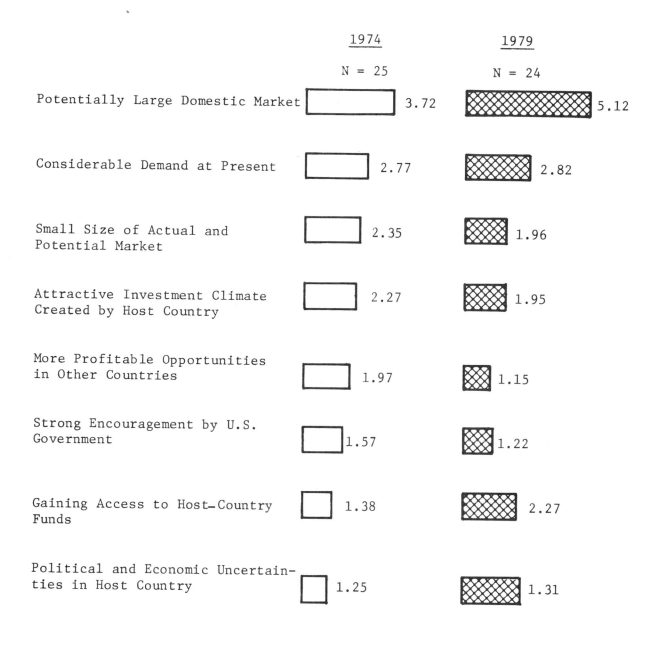

	1974	1979
	N = 25	N = 24
Potentially Large Domestic Market	3.72	5.12
Considerable Demand at Present	2.77	2.82
Small Size of Actual and Potential Market	2.35	1.96
Attractive Investment Climate Created by Host Country	2.27	1.95
More Profitable Opportunities in Other Countries	1.97	1.15
Strong Encouragement by U.S. Government	1.57	1.22
Gaining Access to Host-Country Funds	1.38	2.27
Political and Economic Uncertainties in Host Country	1.25	1.31

is presented in Graph 7, for Iran, Egypt, and Saudi Arabia.

A significant majority of the respondents consider the host government in Iran to be very stable at present; none of the respondents considers the Iranian government to be unstable at present. In five years, companies perceive a marked reduction in the very stable category and an increase in the moderately stable category.

Graph 8 presents several reasons which might promote or reduce the stability of a government. In the case of Iran, both at present and in five years, the predominant reason for government stability is economic stability. Consolidation of power by political leaders and a greater sense of national unity are stated in descending order of frequency. Considerations detrimental to governmental stability are accorded limited weight by the responding companies.

The stability of the Egyptian government in the eyes of the responding companies is significantly different from the case of Iran (Graph 7). The vast majority of responding companies consider the Egyptian government at present to be moderately stable; the response pattern does not reveal much of a change in five years.

Graph 9 offers a combination of reasons promoting and hindering government stability in Egypt. At present, the potential for armed conflict is both contributory and unfavorable to government stability. It is contributory to the extent that it creates a greater sense of national unity and might assist in consolidation of power by political leaders. It is unfavorable to government stability since armed conflict absorbs scarce resources which otherwise might be available for broader-based economic development of the country. Responding companies suggest two broad themes influencing governmental stability

36

GRAPH 7

DISTRIBUTION OF RESPONDENTS' OPINIONS OF STABILITY OF
SELECTED MIDDLE EASTERN GOVERNMENTS - 1974 AND 1979

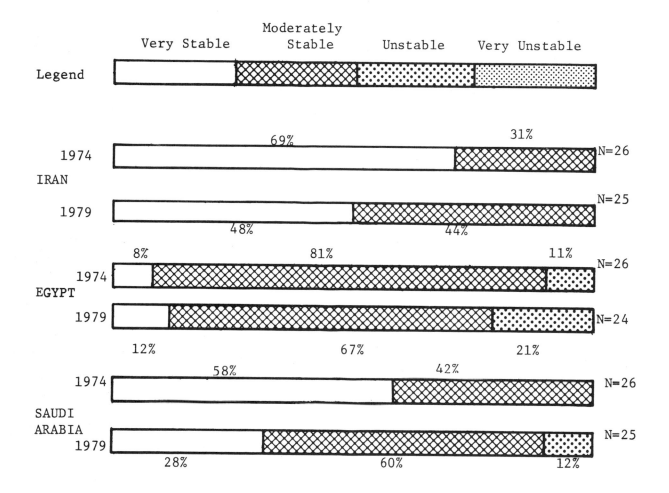

GRAPH 8

MAIN REASONS FOR RESPONDENTS' OPINIONS OF
STABILITY OF IRAN'S GOVERNMENT - 1974 AND 1979

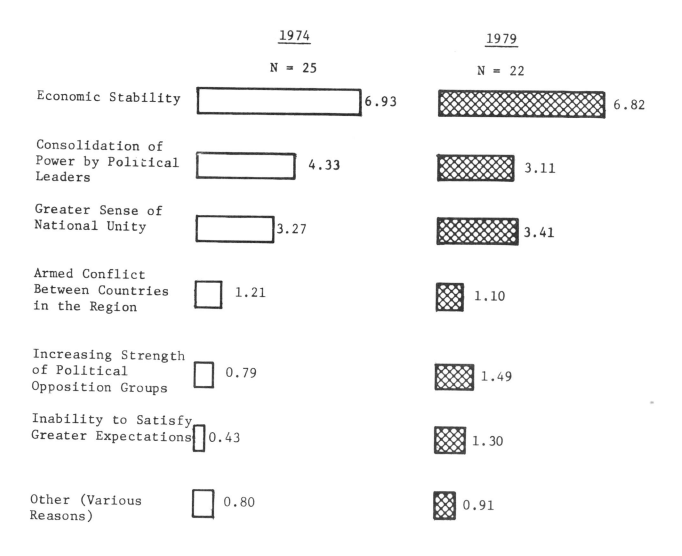

GRAPH 9

MAIN REASONS FOR RESPONDENTS' OPINIONS OF
STABILITY OF EGYPT'S GOVERNMENT - 1974 AND 1979

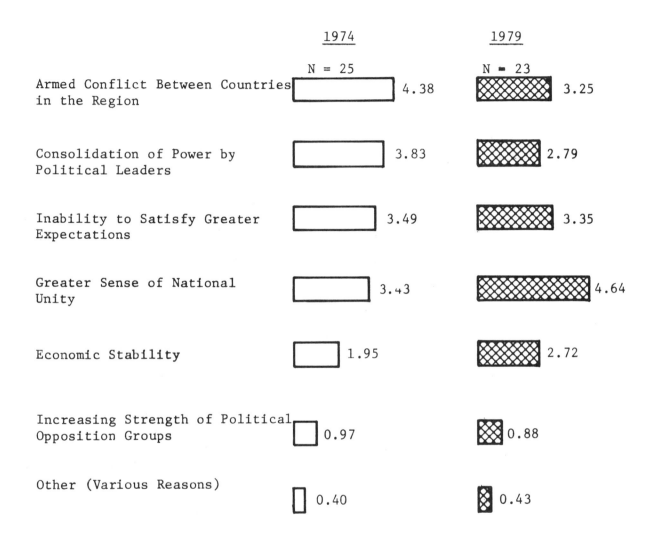

1974   1979

N = 25   N = 23

Armed Conflict Between Countries in the Region   4.38   3.25

Consolidation of Power by Political Leaders   3.83   2.79

Inability to Satisfy Greater Expectations   3.49   3.35

Greater Sense of National Unity   3.43   4.64

Economic Stability   1.95   2.72

Increasing Strength of Political Opposition Groups   0.97   0.88

Other (Various Reasons)   0.40   0.43

over the next five years: potential of armed conflict and ability to satisfy better the economic expectations of the people.

A majority of the responding companies views the Saudi Arabian government as very stable at present followed by moderately stable (Graph 7). None of the respondents considers the host government to be unstable. However, in five years, the largest response category is moderately stable followed by very stable; a small minority expects instability.

Graph 10 shows that economic stability is considered to be the major reason for governmental stability at present and in five years, followed by consolidation of power by political leaders. Greater sense of national unity ranked third at present shifts to second position in five years.

Extent of Foreign Ownership. As foreign direct investments of American companies in the Middle East increase, there will be growing attention given to the question of extent of foreign ownership allowed by the host country. This issue has figured prominently in the policies of U.S. companies in other developing countries. Graph 11 presents the views of the responding executives on the extent of foreign ownership they expect the host countries (Iran, Egypt, and Saudi Arabia) to permit at present and in five years.

By far the largest response category for Iran at present is minority foreign ownership, followed at some distance by 100% foreign ownership. Majority foreign ownership and 50-50 foreign and domestic ownership are given given as responses from 13% of

GRAPH 10

MAIN REASONS FOR RESPONDENTS' OPINIONS OF STABILITY
OF SAUDI ARABIA'S GOVERNMENT - 1974 AND 1979

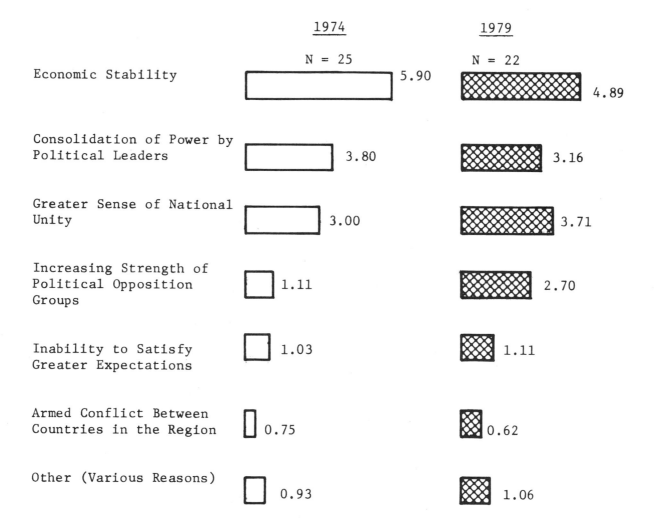

GRAPH 11

RESPONDENTS' OPINIONS OF HOST GOVERNMENTS' ATTITUDE
TOWARD FOREIGN OWNERSHIP – 1974 AND 1979

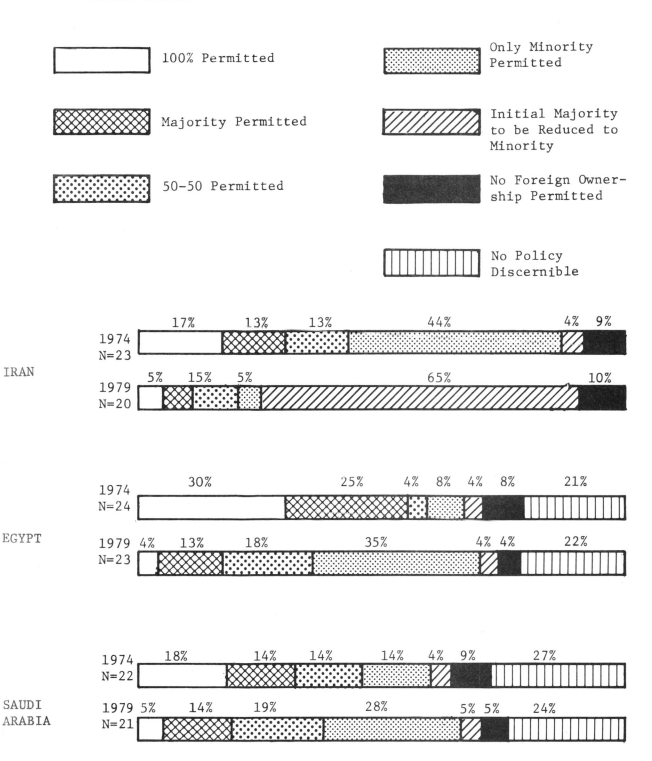

the respondents. A small percentage (9%) suggests that at the present time the host government does not have a discernible policy.

In five years, the respondents expect significant changes in the ownership policies of the Iranian government. Thus, a significant majority (65%) expect the host country to permit only minority foreign ownership. This is followed at some distance by majority foreign ownership (15%) and initial foreign majority reduced to minority over time (10%). A mere 5% of the respondents feel that 100% foreign ownership will be permitted in five years. In brief, the predominant pattern in five years will be of joint ventures, with the foreign company holding a minority equity position. These companies want to benefit from Iran's huge expenditures, and this encourages them to accept a far higher level of discomfort than would be true in a country such as India.

Graph 12 offers some of the reasons for the Iranian government's attitude and policies on foreign ownership as perceived by the responding companies. In general, the most important reason is the stronger bargaining position of the host country vis-à-vis foreign companies. Nationalistic considerations require at least the appearance of financial control by host-country nationals, a reason ranked second by the respondents. Pressure by local businessmen on the host government for reduction of foreign ownership is not deemed to be of significance in comparison to the other reasons at present or in five years. U.S. companies might be forced to accept minority foreign ownership because companies from other countries (notably Japan) are willing to accept minority participation.

GRAPH 12

REASONS FOR IRANIAN GOVERNMENT'S ATTITUDE ON
EXTENT OF FOREIGN OWNERSHIP - 1974 AND 1979

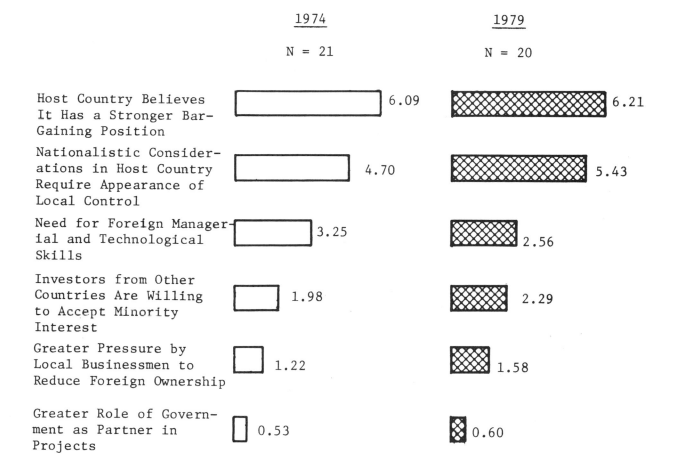

1974

N = 21

1979

N = 20

Host Country Believes It Has a Stronger Bar-Gaining Position — 6.09 — 6.21

Nationalistic Considerations in Host Country Require Appearance of Local Control — 4.70 — 5.43

Need for Foreign Managerial and Technological Skills — 3.25 — 2.56

Investors from Other Countries Are Willing to Accept Minority Interest — 1.98 — 2.29

Greater Pressure by Local Businessmen to Reduce Foreign Ownership — 1.22 — 1.58

Greater Role of Government as Partner in Projects — 0.53 — 0.60

GRAPH 13

REASONS FOR EGYPTIAN GOVERNMENT'S ATTITUDES
ON EXTENT OF FOREIGN OWNERSHIP – 1974 AND 1979

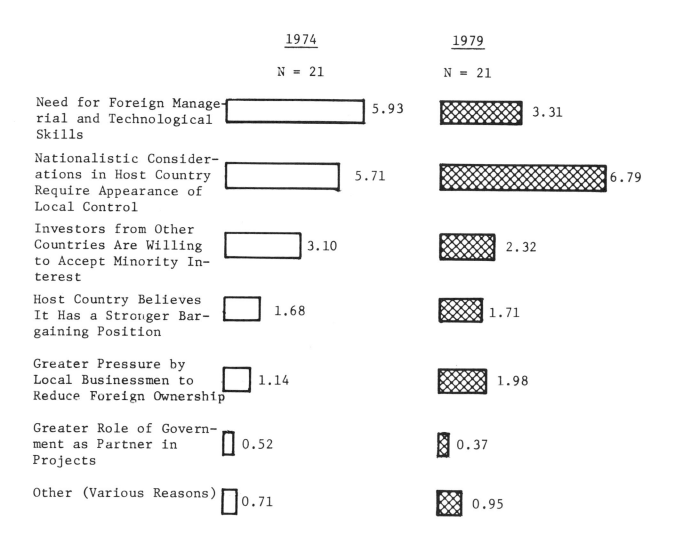

	1974	1979
	N = 21	N = 21
Need for Foreign Managerial and Technological Skills	5.93	3.31
Nationalistic Considerations in Host Country Require Appearance of Local Control	5.71	6.79
Investors from Other Countries Are Willing to Accept Minority Interest	3.10	2.32
Host Country Believes It Has a Stronger Bargaining Position	1.68	1.71
Greater Pressure by Local Businessmen to Reduce Foreign Ownership	1.14	1.98
Greater Role of Government as Partner in Projects	0.52	0.37
Other (Various Reasons)	0.71	0.95

Graph 11 shows that the category most frequently referred to for Egypt is 100% foreign ownership followed by majority ownership. However, a significant minority (22%) of the respondents feel that there is no discernible policy at present, referring to the lack of precedents. Limiting foreign ownership to a minority position is listed by a very small percentage of the respondents.

In five years, the response pattern shows significant changes. The largest response category becomes minority foreign ownership (35%) followed by 22% who feel that even at that time there will not be a discernible policy; 18% feel that 50-50 ownership combinations will be allowed, whereas 13% believe that the host government will permit majority foreign ownership.

Graph 13 shows the relative ranking of reasons for the particular policies toward foreign ownership by Egypt. Need for foreign managerial and technical skills are ranked the highest at present, which partially explains Egypt's attitude toward extent of ownership. However, several other considerations do not favor significant foreign ownership. Nationalistic considerations are of extreme importance in limiting foreign ownership and control. Additionally, non-U.S. investors are willing to accept minority equity interest which permits the host country to negotiate with U.S. investors.

In five years, nationalistic considerations requiring local control are viewed as by far the most important consideration in the Egyptian government's policies toward foreign ownership. Need for foreign managerial and technical skills shows a perceptible decrease in relative scores. The remaining reasons are generally consistent with the pattern at present.

GRAPH 14

REASONS FOR SAUDI ARABIAN GOVERNMENT'S ATTITUDES ON
EXTENT OF FOREIGN OWNERSHIP - 1974 AND 1979

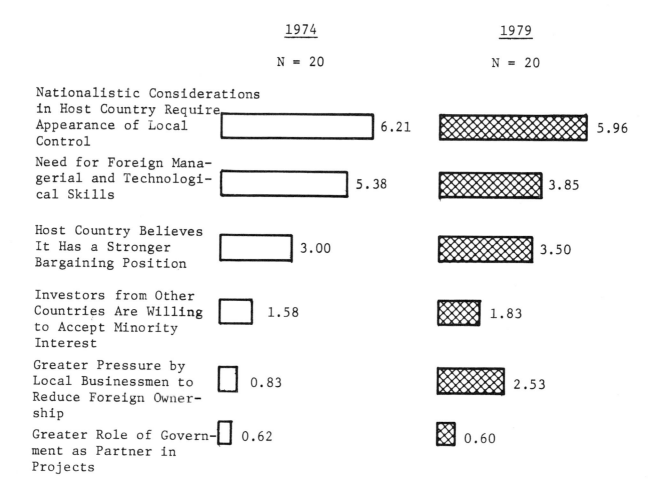

At present, the highest response category for Saudi Arabia
is for "no discernible policy" (27%) followed by 100% ownership
(18%) and 14% for each of the categories on "majority," "50-50,"
and "only minority" ownership (Graph 11).

The response pattern for 1979 shows changes. The largest
response category is of "only minority" ownership (28%) followed
by "no policy discernible" (24%), "50-50" (19%), and "majority"
foreign ownership (14%). A mere 5% feel that 100% foreign ownership will still be possible.

Graph 14 offers some of the reasons for the foreign ownership policies of the host government. The relative ranking of
reasons at present and in five years does not reveal any significant change. The most important reason for limitations on extent
of foreign ownership at present and in five years is that nationalistic considerations require local control. Managerial and technical skills of the foreign company can be secured without vio-
lating ownership policy preferences of Saudi Arabia, because of
the stronger bargaining position of the host country and the
willingness of non-U.S. companies to accept a minority interest.

The growing pressure of local businessmen on limiting foreign
ownership shows a marked growth compared to its ranking at present.
This suggests a growing role and influence of the indigenous businessman in the plans and policies of the home government, and also
implies that the objectives of local partners on this and other
points might be quite different from those of his foreign partner.

Major Operating Problems. Graph 15 identifies the major operating

problems envisioned by U.S. companies in Iran at present and in five years. By far the most serious operating problem at present and in five years for the responding companies is the lack of qualified nationals followed by the lack of industrial and business experience on the part of host-country government officials. Graft and corruption as part of the process of doing business in Iran is noted as the third most significant problem at present and in five years, followed by a lack of well-defined policies on investment and development of Iran. The respondents *do not* feel that some of their problems might be due to limitations in their own organization (in terms of structure and orientation) to serve the changing market needs of Iran. Thus, the major operating problems are viewed as being largely external to the organization.

While lack of qualified nationals is viewed as the most important operating problem in Egypt at present and in five years, lack of well-defined policies of the host country occupies second position, which changes slightly (to third ranking) in five years (Graph 16). Lack of industrial and business experience on the part of host-government officials, especially in terms of private enterprise, is ranked third at present but escalates to second rank in five years. Graft and corruption on the part of host-country officials is ranked as number four at present and in five years. Under the category of "other," financial problems of the Egyptian government are noted as an important operating constraint. Again, as in the case of Iran, the company's organization structure and orientation for doing business in Egypt is not viewed as a significant reason for experiencing operating problems.

GRAPH 15

MAJOR PROBLEMS OF OPERATING
IN IRAN – 1974 AND 1979

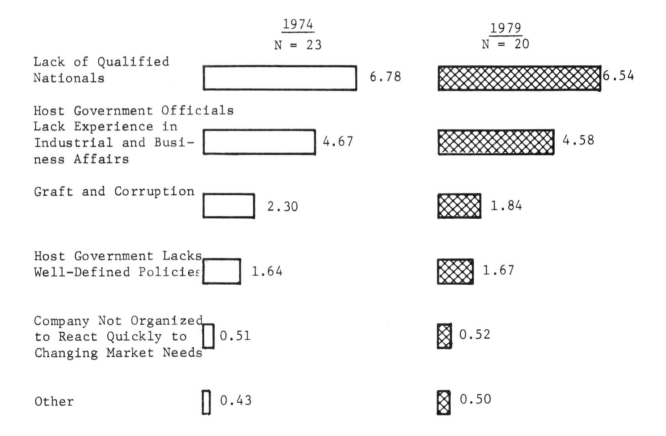

GRAPH 16

MAJOR PROBLEMS OF OPERATING
IN EGYPT - 1974 AND 1979

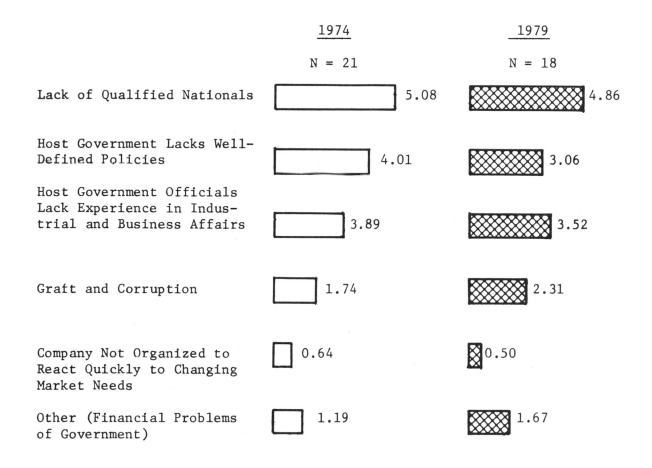

	1974	1979
	N = 21	N = 18
Lack of Qualified Nationals	5.08	4.86
Host Government Lacks Well-Defined Policies	4.01	3.06
Host Government Officials Lack Experience in Industrial and Business Affairs	3.89	3.52
Graft and Corruption	1.74	2.31
Company Not Organized to React Quickly to Changing Market Needs	0.64	0.50
Other (Financial Problems of Government)	1.19	1.67

In the case of Saudi Arabia, by far the most important operating problem at present and in five years is the lack of qualified natio- als, followed by (in descending order both for the present and in five years) lack of business and industrial experience, lack of well-defined policies, and graft and corruption (Graph 17).

In general, therefore, for all three countries, the major oper- ating problem stated by the responding companies is lack of qualified host-country national, lack of business and industrial experience by host-government officials, followed by lack of clearly-defined policies. Of course, these and other characteristics of operations will have a bearing on the pace at which foreign companies can undertake and deliver on their projects.

Extent of Foreign Competition. Companies from Europe, Japan, Eastern Europe, U.S.S.R. and developing countries, in addition to U.S. compa- nies, are converging on the Middle East to participate in and benefit from the development plans of the regions. Graphs 18-23 present the views of responding companies on the main sources and level of com- petition at present and in five years.

For Iran, at present, West Germany is viewed as the strongest competitor, followed by Great Britain and France (co-ranked), Japan, and the Soviet Union (Graph 18). A significant majority of the respondents do not consider the Soviet Union as a source of any competition while a significant minority does not consider Japan as a source of any competition.

However, in five years, the responding companies note changes. West Germany will remain the strongest source of competition; nearly

GRAPH 17

MAJOR PROBLEMS OF OPERATING
IN SAUDI ARABIA - 1974 AND 1979

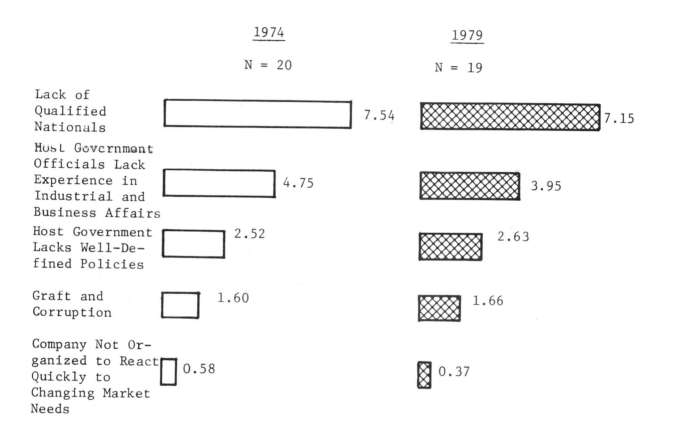

GRAPH 18

MAJOR SOURCES OF FOREIGN COMPETITION FOR U.S. COMPANIES
IN IRAN - 1974 AND 1979

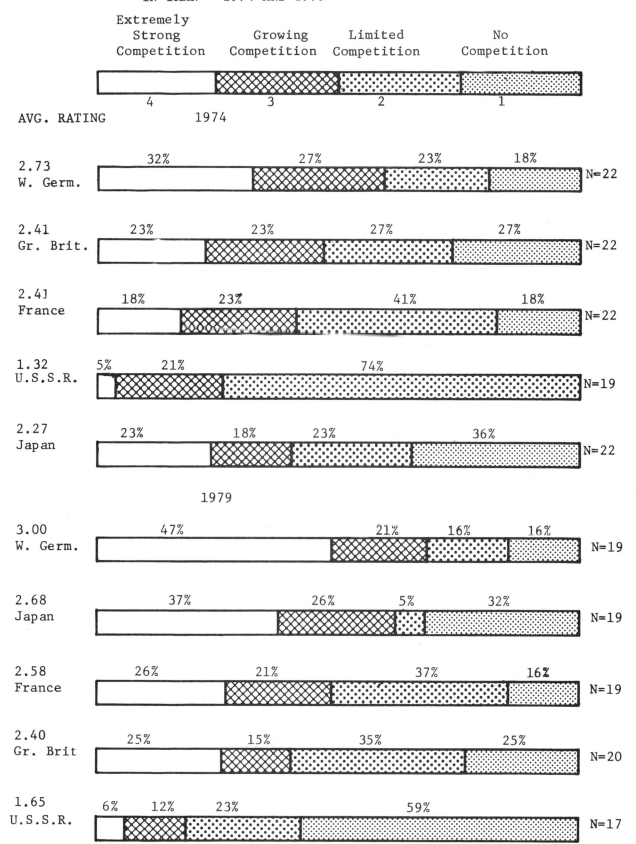

54

50% of the respondents viewed West Germany as offering "extremely strong" competition. Japan shows a significant jump from a rank of fourth at present to a rank of second in five years. The other sources of competition in descending order are France, Great Britain, and the Soviet Union.

Graph 19 offers reasons for the competitive strength of non-U.S. companies in Iran at present and in five years. In the view of the responding companies, the most important reason for the competitive strength of non-U.S. companies is the substantial assistance they receive from their home governments. Other reasons in descending order are: more favorable financing terms; foreign sources are competitive in price and quality; attaching greater importance to the Middle East; and longer history of doing business in Iran.

In five years, responding companies feel that foreign companies will continue to receive substantial assistance from their home governments which will become the second most important reason for their competitive strength. However, the most important reason for competitive strength of non-U.S. companies with U.S. companies in Iran will be because they are competitive in price and quality. More favorable terms of financing by foreign companies slips from second at present to third in five years. The other reasons do not show any significant change in five years.

For Egypt, at present, West Germany is the strongest competitor followed by Great Britain, France, Japan, and the U.S.S.R. (Graph 20). In five years, West Germany is still the strongest competitor, but Japan has moved into second position, followed by France, Great Britain, and the Soviet Union. As in the case of Iran, West Germany

GRAPH 19

MAIN REASONS FOR FOREIGN COMPETITION
IN IRAN - 1974 AND 1979

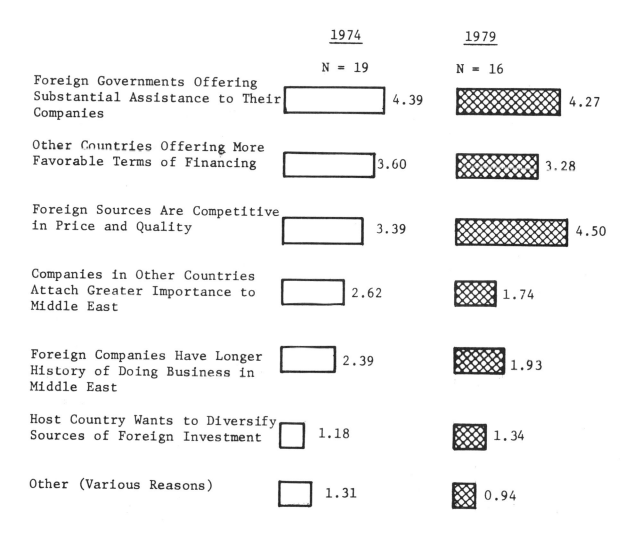

GRAPH 20

MAJOR SOURCES OF FOREIGN COMPETITION IN EGYPT - 1974 AND 1979

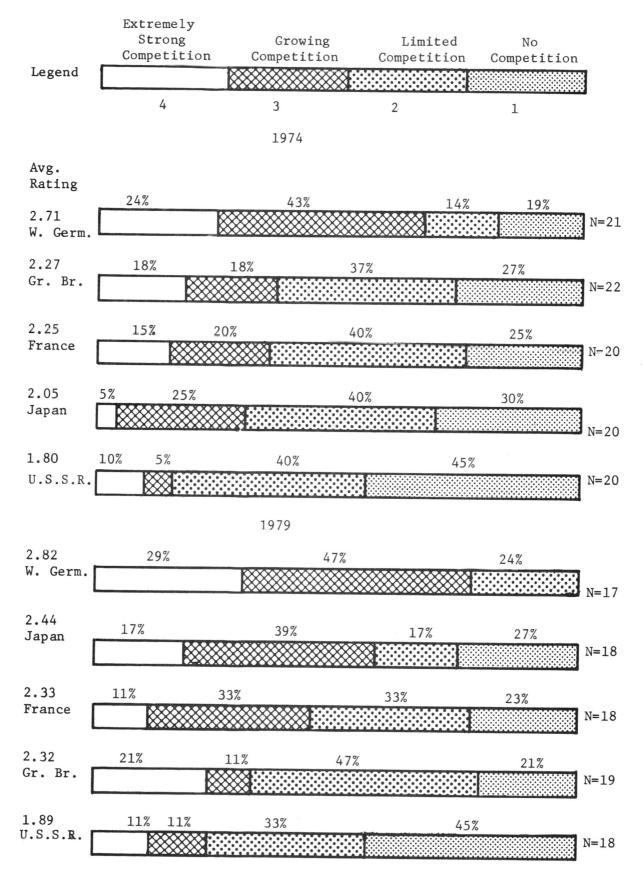

and Japan emerge as the top two competitors for U.S. companies.

The relative ranking of the main reasons at present for the competitive strength of non-U.S. companies in Egypt is not significantly different from the ranking for Iran (Graph 21). The assistance received by foreign companies from their home governments is considered as the most important reason of competitive strength at present.

In five years, as in the case of Iran, the most important reason for competitive strength of non-U.S. companies will be due to their being competitive in terms of price and quality. The remaining reasons are ranked similar to the response for Iran.

For Saudi Arabia, at present, West Germany is the strongest source of competition followed by Great Britain, France, Japan, and the Soviet Union (Graph 22). In five years, the ranking changes to (in descending order) West Germany, Japan, Great Britain, France, and the Soviet Union. As in Iran and Egypt, West Germany and Japan emerge as the top two competitors for U.S. companies.

The main reasons for competitive strength show variations from the pattern noted for Iran and Egypt (Graph 23). By far the most important reason for competitive strength of non-U.S. companies is the substantial assistance of their home governments. The remaining reasons for competitive strength follow at a considerable distance and reflect rankings which are not different from those of Iran and Egypt.

In five years, the most important reason remains the assistance by the home government of foreign companies. This is followed by competitiveness in price and quality, more favorable terms of

GRAPH 21

MAIN REASONS FOR FOREIGN COMPETITION
IN EGYPT - 1974 AND 1979

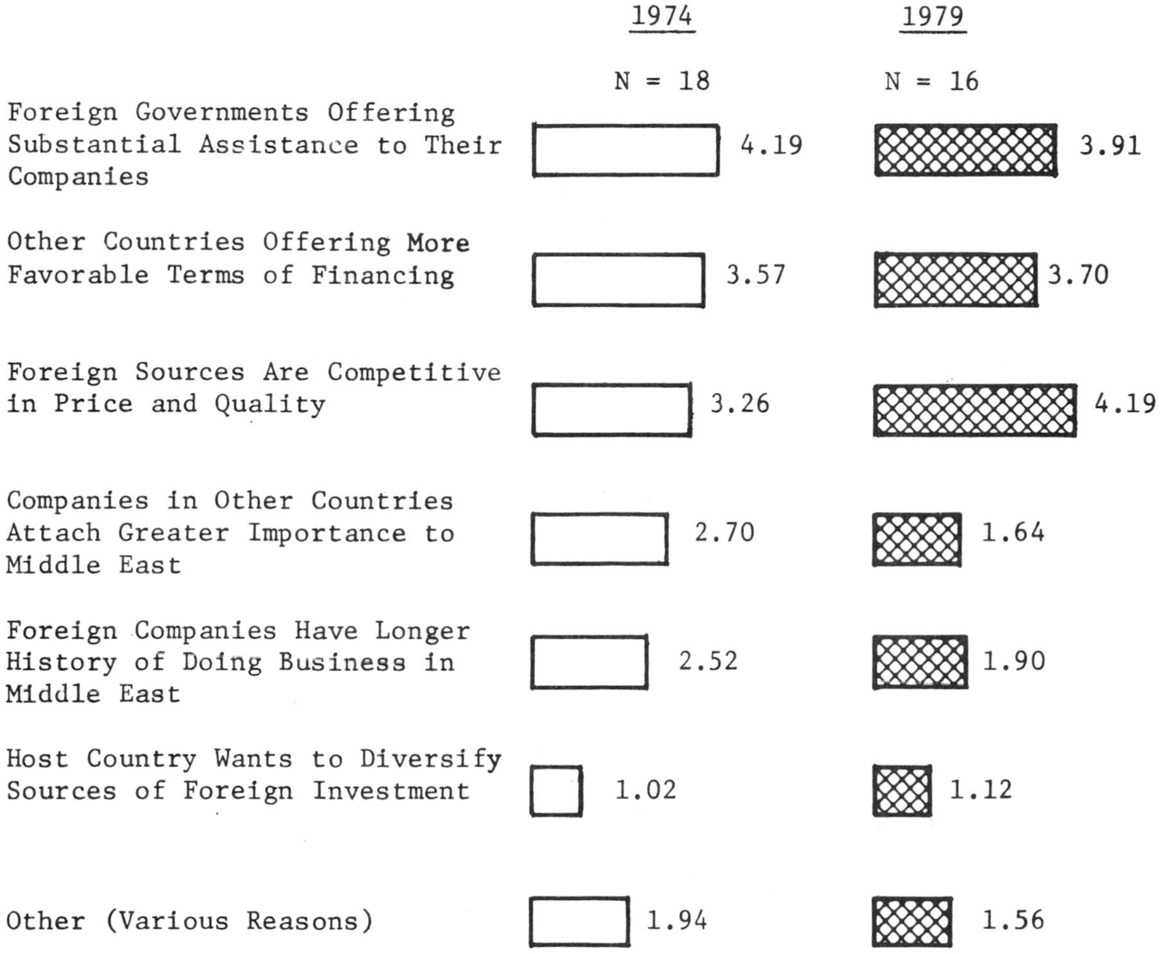

	1974	1979
	N = 18	N = 16
Foreign Governments Offering Substantial Assistance to Their Companies	4.19	3.91
Other Countries Offering More Favorable Terms of Financing	3.57	3.70
Foreign Sources Are Competitive in Price and Quality	3.26	4.19
Companies in Other Countries Attach Greater Importance to Middle East	2.70	1.64
Foreign Companies Have Longer History of Doing Business in Middle East	2.52	1.90
Host Country Wants to Diversify Sources of Foreign Investment	1.02	1.12
Other (Various Reasons)	1.94	1.56

59

GRAPH 22

MAJOR SOURCES OF FOREIGN COMPETITION FOR U.S. COMPANIES
IN SAUDI ARABIA - 1974 AND 1979

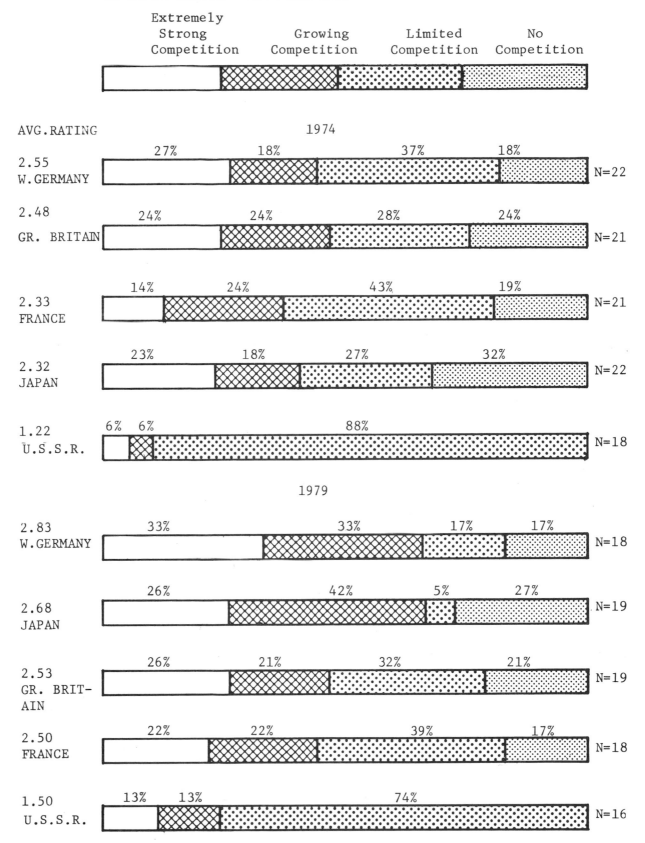

GRAPH 23

MAIN REASONS FOR FOREIGN COMPETITION
IN SAUDI ARABIA - 1974 AND 1979

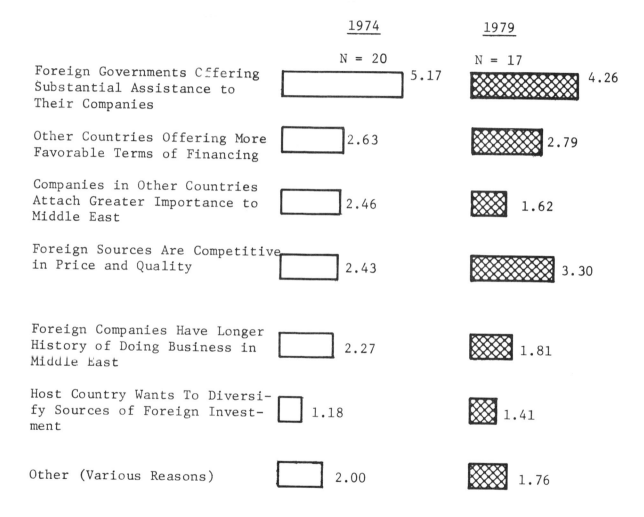

	1974	1979
	N = 20	N = 17
Foreign Governments Cffering Substantial Assistance to Their Companies	5.17	4.26
Other Countries Offering More Favorable Terms of Financing	2.63	2.79
Companies in Other Countries Attach Greater Importance to Middle East	2.46	1.62
Foreign Sources Are Competitive in Price and Quality	2.43	3.30
Foreign Companies Have Longer History of Doing Business in Middle East	2.27	1.81
Host Country Wants To Diversify Sources of Foreign Investment	1.18	1.41
Other (Various Reasons)	2.00	1.76

GRAPH 24

EXPECTED ANNUAL INCREASE OF INVESTMENTS
IN SELECTED MIDDLE EASTERN COUNTRIES

Increase by:

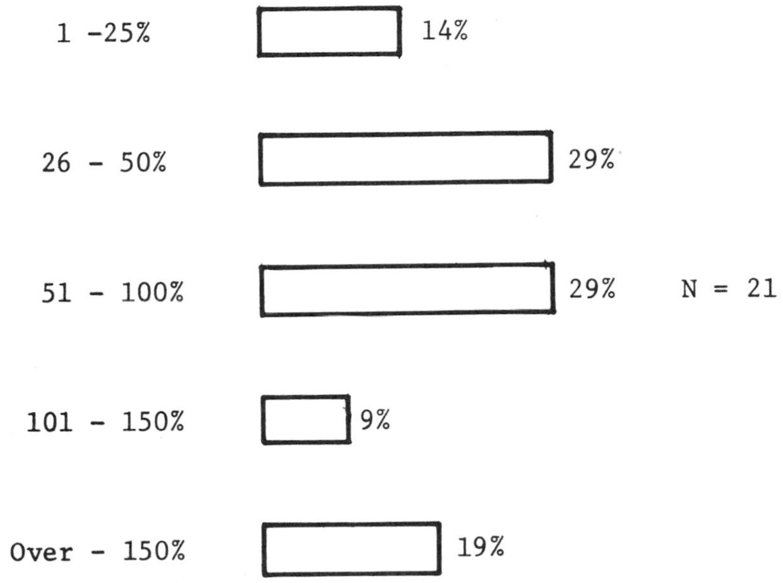

1 -25%   14%

26 - 50%   29%

51 - 100%   29%   N = 21

101 - 150%   9%

Over - 150%   19%

Decrease by :   0%

Remain At Present Level: 0%

GRAPH 25

EXPECTED INCREASE OF INVESTMENTS BY SELECTED
MIDDLE EASTERN COUNTRIES OVER THE NEXT FIVE YEARS

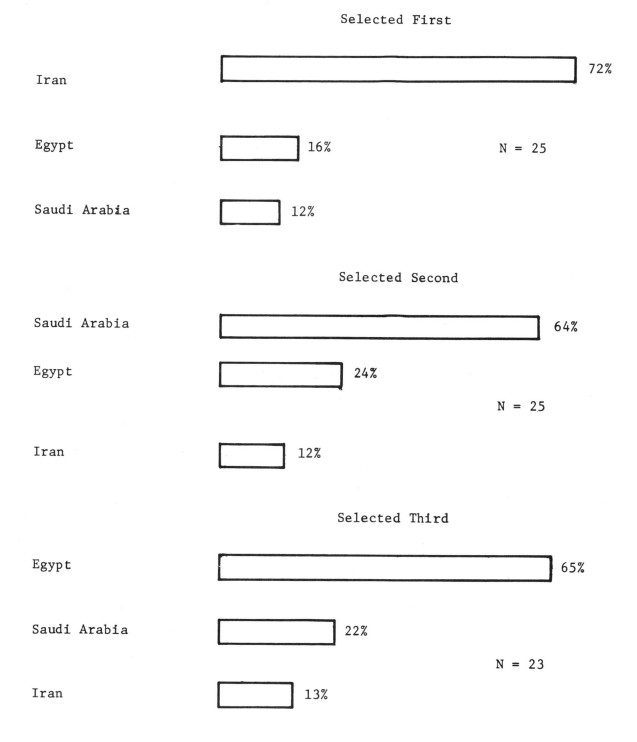

Selected First

Iran   72%

Egypt   16%   N = 25

Saudi Arabia   12%

Selected Second

Saudi Arabia   64%

Egypt   24%

                        N = 25

Iran   12%

Selected Third

Egypt   65%

Saudi Arabia   22%

                        N = 23

Iran   13%

financing, a longer history of doing business in Saudi Arabia, and attaching greater importance to the country.

Extent of Future Investments.   Graph 24 shows the strong and continued interest of companies in the Middle East.   None of the responding companies intends to reduce or merely maintain current investment levels; all of the respondents *intend to increase* their levels of investment. The graph shows that the annual rate of increase over the next five years is distributed as follows: 14% (1-25%); 29% (26-50%);   29% (51-100%);   9% (101-150%); and 19% (over 150%).

Graph 25 present the response on the relative ranking of countries in terms of new investments.   By far the largest first choice is Iran, by 72% of the respondents, followed by Saudi Arabia (64%) as second choice, and Egypt (65%) as third choice.

3

Foreign Investments by Middle Eastern Countries

THIS CHAPTER discusses two questions:

1. In the opinion of responding companies, what are the objectives of the surplus oil revenue countries of the Middle East in investing in the U.S. and in the developing countries of Asia?

2. What role might be played by the U.S. IC in such investment flows?

A brief introduction to the scope of the issue precedes the discussion of these questions.

Even by the most conservative estimates, several member nations of OPEC (Organization of Petroleum Exporting Countries), primarily those from the Middle East, will continue to generate foreign exchange surpluses. The economic position of the oil-importing nations is contingent in many respects on their ability to offset balance of payments deficits with foreign investments by oil-exporting nations. Table 8 sets forth the distribution of surplus oil revenues in 1974.

T A B L E 8

DISTRIBUTION OF 1974 SURPLUS OIL REVENUES

	Billions of $	%
Eurocurrencies	21.0	35.0
United Kingdom Bank Deposits and Government Securities	7.5	12.5
U.S. Government Securities	6.0	10.0
Loans to Developed Countries Other Than U.S. and U.K.	5.5	9.1
U.S. Bank Deposits	4.0	6.7
World Bank and I.M.F. Obligations	3.5	6.0
Loans to Developing Countries	2.5	4.0
U.S. Stocks and Other Equity	1.0	1.7
Miscellaneous (Including Private Loans, European and Japanese Securities)	9.0	15.0
	60.0	100.0

Source: Estimated by U.S. Treasury Department as published in *Newsweek,* February 10, 1975.

INVESTMENT OBJECTIVES IN THE U.S.

According to the respondent companies, the objectives of the Middle East oil-producing countries in investing their surplus revenues in the U.S. are stated in Graph 26 for Iran and Graph 27 for Arab oil producers.

Iran's primary objective at present is to secure a safe return--e.g., invest in U.S. Government securities (Graph 26). Of secondary importance, in descending order, is to associate with U.S. companies for investment in third countries, and to invest in real estate. A significant minority feel that Iran does not know what it wants to do with its surplus revenue. To buy shares of U.S. companies and to gain controlling interest in them are not considered important objectives.

By 1979, securing a safe return, though ranked first, is expected to be of lesser relative importance. It is felt that Iran will place greater emphasis on buying shares of U.S. companies, though not necessarily in gaining a controlling interest. To associate with U.S. companies for investment in third countries is ranked third. This objective remains important for Iran in the opinion of responding companies.

Like Iran, the primary objective of the Arab oil producers investing their surplus revenues in the U.S. is to secure a safe return (Graph 27). Investing in real estate is ranked second.

There is some contention that Middle East producers do not know what they want to do with their surplus revenues To associate with U.S. companies for investment in third countries is not considered to be a significant objective at present. To gain a controlling interest

GRAPH 26

OBJECTIVES OF IRAN IN INVESTING SURPLUS REVENUES
IN THE U.S. – 1974 AND 1979

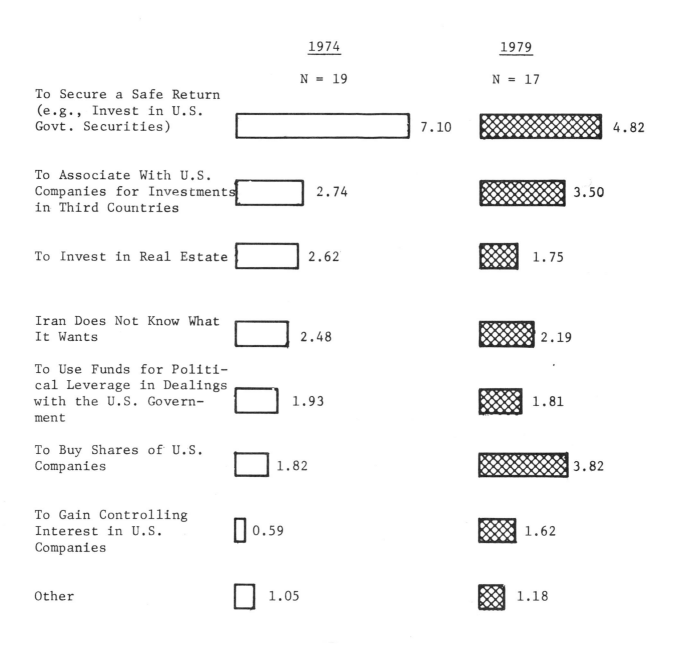

<u>1974</u>   <u>1979</u>

N = 19   N = 17

To Secure a Safe Return
(e.g., Invest in U.S.
Govt. Securities)   7.10   4.82

To Associate With U.S.
Companies for Investments   2.74   3.50
in Third Countries

To Invest in Real Estate   2.62   1.75

Iran Does Not Know What
It Wants   2.48   2.19

To Use Funds for Politi-
cal Leverage in Dealings
with the U.S. Govern-   1.93   1.81
ment

To Buy Shares of U.S.
Companies   1.82   3.82

To Gain Controlling
Interest in U.S.   0.59   1.62
Companies

Other   1.05   1.18

GRAPH 27

OBJECTIVES OF ARAB OIL-PRODUCING COUNTRIES
IN INVESTING SURPLUS REVENUES
IN THE U.S. - 1974 AND 1979

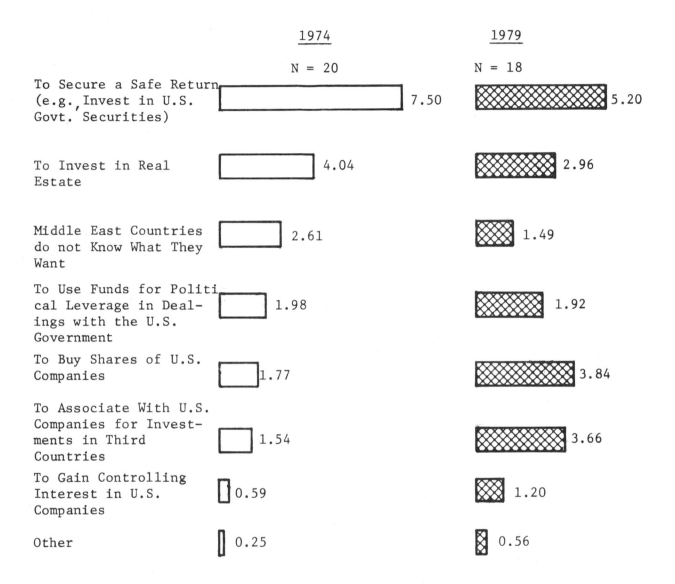

	1974	1979
	N = 20	N = 18
To Secure a Safe Return (e.g., Invest in U.S. Govt. Securities)	7.50	5.20
To Invest in Real Estate	4.04	2.96
Middle East Countries do not Know What They Want	2.61	1.49
To Use Funds for Political Leverage in Dealings with the U.S. Government	1.98	1.92
To Buy Shares of U.S. Companies	1.77	3.84
To Associate With U.S. Companies for Investments in Third Countries	1.54	3.66
To Gain Controlling Interest in U.S. Companies	0.59	1.20
Other	0.25	0.56

in U.S. companies has the lowest ranking of all choices at present.

The projected pattern of objectives of foreign investment in five years, however, reflects changes from the existing pattern. While securing a safe return is still the most important objective, buying shares of U.S. companies is viewed as the second most important objective, followed by associating with U.S. companies for investing in third countries. Gaining controlling interest of U.S. companies is not considered to be a significant objective.

INVESTMENT OBJECTIVES IN ASIA

The developing countries have been severely affected by increases in crude oil prices, as demonstrated by studies of the World Bank. They need foreign exchange as one of the key inputs in proceeding with their development programs. The surplus oil revenue countries, especially the Arab countries of the Gulf, possess surplus revenues. Some part of these surpluses will find their way to the developing countries for economic, political, military, religious, and humanitarian reasons.

Graphs 28 and 29 present the views of responding companies regarding the objectives of Iran and Arab oil-producing countries, respectively, in investing in Asia. At present, the most important objective is to forge closer political ties with Asian countries through economic actions, including investments. This objective is followed by others in descending order of importance: diversification of investments to spread risks, and gaining access to Asian technical and managerial skills. Religious and humanitarian considerations are also noted but are secondary to the economic and political considerations.

GRAPH 28

OBJECTIVES OF IRAN IN INVESTING IN THE
DEVELOPING COUNTRIES OF ASIA - 1974 AND 1979

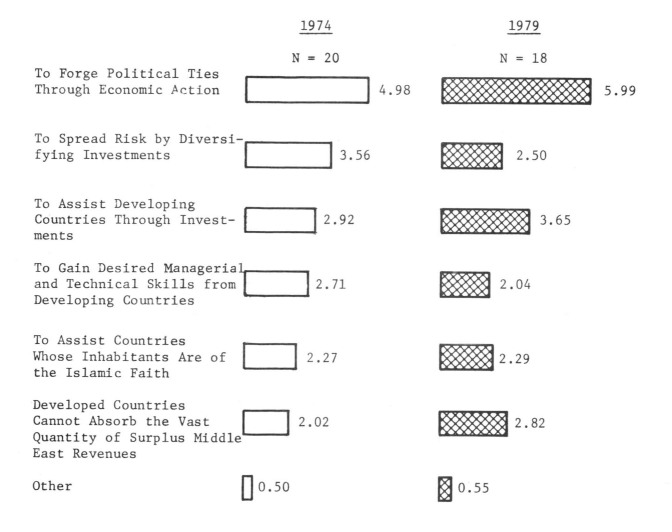

	1974	1979
	N = 20	N = 18
To Forge Political Ties Through Economic Action	4.98	5.99
To Spread Risk by Diversifying Investments	3.56	2.50
To Assist Developing Countries Through Investments	2.92	3.65
To Gain Desired Managerial and Technical Skills from Developing Countries	2.71	2.04
To Assist Countries Whose Inhabitants Are of the Islamic Faith	2.27	2.29
Developed Countries Cannot Absorb the Vast Quantity of Surplus Middle East Revenues	2.02	2.82
Other	0.50	0.55

GRAPH 29

OBJECTIVES OF ARAB OIL-PRODUCING COUNTRIES IN INVESTING
IN THE DEVELOPING COUNTRIES OF ASIA – 1974 AND 1979

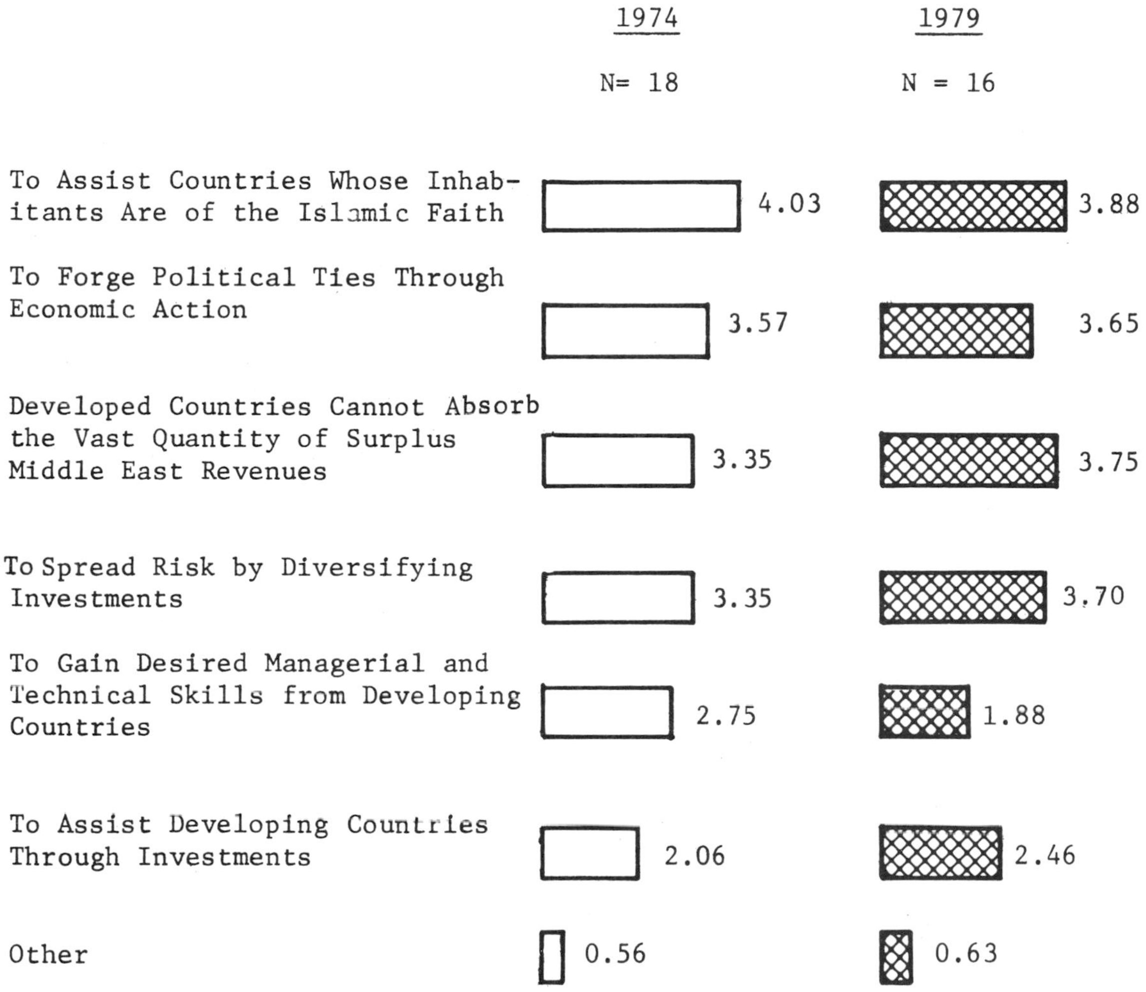

	1974 N= 18	1979 N = 16
To Assist Countries Whose Inhabitants Are of the Islamic Faith	4.03	3.88
To Forge Political Ties Through Economic Action	3.57	3.65
Developed Countries Cannot Absorb the Vast Quantity of Surplus Middle East Revenues	3.35	3.75
To Spread Risk by Diversifying Investments	3.35	3.70
To Gain Desired Managerial and Technical Skills from Developing Countries	2.75	1.88
To Assist Developing Countries Through Investments	2.06	2.46
Other	0.56	0.63

In five years, respondents expect some changes in relative ranking of objectives. To forge political ties through economic actions remains the most important by far. The second ranking objective is assisting developing countries (mainly Asian and Arab) through investments. Of course, the first two objectives are closely related and synergistic. However, economic considerations also remain important through diversifying risks and gaining access to managerial and technical skills. In brief, with the passage of time, the respondents visualize relatively greater stress by Iran on political-economic dimensions when investing in Asia.

The relative ranking of objectives of the Arab oil-producing countries at present and in five years is presented in Graph 29. At present, the religious factor is considered to be the most important objective leading to investments in Asian countries with large Muslim populations--such as Pakistan, Bangladesh, Malaysia, and Indonesia. A close second is the objective of forging political ties through economic actions. (This objective is related to religious and humanitarian objectives.) However, economic considerations are also important as they serve to promote political objectives, spread investment risks, and gain managerial and technical skills sorely needed in the Arab oil-producing countries.

The relative ranking of the response for five years hence is not significantly different from the pattern stated for the present. In contrast to Iran, respondents expect the religious factor to play a greater role in the investment objectives of the Arab oil producers.

GRAPH 30

ROLE OF AMERICAN COMPANIES IN ASSISTING
IRAN AND SAUDI ARABIA IN INVESTING SURPLUS REVENUES
IN THE DEVELOPING COUNTRIES OF ASIA

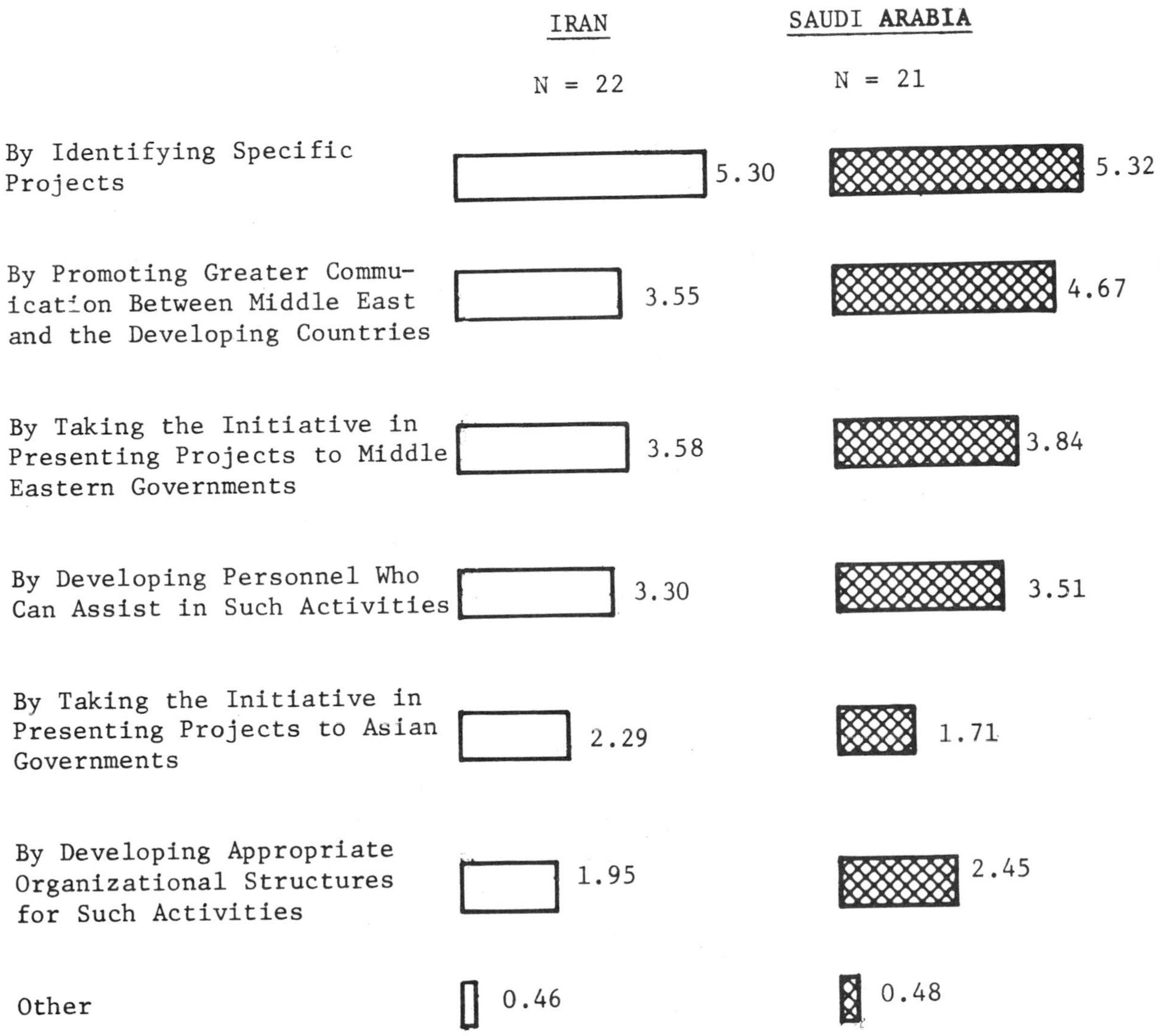

	IRAN	SAUDI ARABIA
	N = 22	N = 21
By Identifying Specific Projects	5.30	5.32
By Promoting Greater Communication Between Middle East and the Developing Countries	3.55	4.67
By Taking the Initiative in Presenting Projects to Middle Eastern Governments	3.58	3.84
By Developing Personnel Who Can Assist in Such Activities	3.30	3.51
By Taking the Initiative in Presenting Projects to Asian Governments	2.29	1.71
By Developing Appropriate Organizational Structures for Such Activities	1.95	2.45
Other	0.46	0.48

Graph 30 offers the relative ranking of ways in which the American company can assist Iran and Saudi Arabia in investing in Asia. The response, however, has relevance for the role of the American company in such investments beyond Asia.

For Iran, by far the greatest importance at present is attached to identification of specific projects by American companies in which Middle Eastern countries could participate. Respondents add that companies should take the initiative in presenting projects to Middle Eastern governments. This approach is viewed within the broader framework of promoting greater communication between the Middle East and the developing countries. However, flows of investments from the Middle East to developing countries (including those in Asia) are a recent possibility. Consequently, the respondents stress that companies wishing to effectively assist on a long-term basis in such flows will have to develop personnel with the proper orientation and skills. Respondents also note that companies will need to develop appropriate organizational structures if they are to assist in such flows.

It should be mentioned that at present respondents attach relatively lower importance to taking the initiative in presenting projects involving Iranian and Arab interests to potential host Asian countries. By this, companies are suggesting that primary attention should be directed toward those with the money rather than those seeking the money.

Graph 30 shows that the overall pattern of response for Saudi Arabia is not significantly different from Iran. In general, the

response indicates that companies anticipate a stronger Saudi Arabian need for specificity and initiative, along with greater stress on personnel and organizational orientation.

4

Planning Business Development in the New Middle East

THE INTERNATIONAL BUSINESS scene is characterized by change and uncertainty as demonstrated by events of the past few years. It is safe to assume that change and uncertainty in the next decade, especially in the new Middle East, **are** likely to be even greater than in the past. Therefore, the essential task for the international business executive, especially in the context of planning business development in the new Middle East, will be to attempt to anticipate the unfolding scenarios being created by change and uncertainty.

This chapter summarizes the views of U.S. companies on the foreign investment climate in Iran, Egypt, and Saudi Arabia (**Section** 1), outlines the concept of the investment life cycle as an approach to planning for business development and operations in the Middle East (Section 2), and highlights major strategic planning considerations and action programs for the IC (Section 3).

SECTION 1: FOREIGN INVESTMENT CLIMATE

U.S. companies have had limited experience in doing business in the Middle East. Yet, the sudden emergence of rich markets and the desire of the U.S. corporation, along with companies from other

parts of the world, to benefit from catering to these markets are forcing companies to make judgments of what is likely to be the foreign investment climate in the coming five years and longer. Subjective opinions and expectations are playing as important a role as any objective analysis (which at this stage is notably absent).

This section summarizes the response of U.S. companies surveyed toward the foreign investment climate in Iran, Egypt, and Saudi Arabia. Observations based on this response can be made for other Middle Eastern countries and for non-U.S. companies. Thus, this summary presents an initial compilation of attitudes which can serve as a basis for a discussion of the complex and changing environment for investment.

Summary of Response. The results of this survey can be briefly summarized:

1. The *existing level of operations* of U.S. companies in the Middle East are essentially at a low level of commitment—in the form of distributorships and representatives. Local manufacturing for the host-country market exists only to a limited extent.

2. The *key objective* of companies at present and in five years is to develop new export markets in Middle Eastern countries. The anticipated growth of local manufacturing, especially in the case of Iran, is almost invariably for host-country markets and not for exports. Companies are entering Middle Eastern markets also to keep up with moves of competitors from the U.S. and elsewhere.

3. Companies anticipate repidly growing *interest* in the Middle East in the next five years because of the existing and potential demand and the ability to pay in foreign exchange, especially by Iran and Saudi Arabia. In the context of Egypt, potential demand is the primary reason for companies' interest.

4. The Iranian and Saudi Arabian *governments are expected to remain stable* over the next five years primarily because of their economic stability, their ability to satisfy rising economic expectations of the people, and the consolidation of power by political leaders. The Egyptian government is viewed as being moderately stable over the next five years mainly because of the potential of armed conflict, which will limit the government's ability to cater to the economic expectations of its people.

5. Joint ventures with *minority foreign ownership* are expected to be the predominant pattern of foreign investment in Iran. The host country is viewed as having the necessary bargaining strength to gain acceptance of its policy on foreign ownership from U.S. and other international companies. Egypt is also expected to stress joint ventures which favor the local partner in terms of ownership interest, mainly for nationalistic considerations. Likewise, Saudi Arabia is expected to place greater weight on joint ventures (although to a somewhat lesser extent than in Iran and Egypt) largely because of nationalistic considerations and the strong bargaining position of the host country.

6. The major *operating problems* in Iran, Egypt, and Saudi Arabia

at present and in five years are lack of qualified host-country nationals, limited experience in business and industrial affairs by host-government officials and local businessmen, and lack of well-defined policies on development and foreign investment. The relative intensity of these problems reflects some variation between these countries. For example, lack of qualified nationals is particularly severe in Saudi Arabia.

7. U.S. companies expect particularly *strong competition* from West Germany and Japan in selling to and investing in the Middle East. The main reasons for the competitive strength of non-U.S. companies in Middle Eastern markets are the support of their home governments (particularly in dealing with Saudi Arabia), competitiveness in terms of price and technology, and realization by the home governments of these companies of the great importance of raw materials and end markets in the region.

8. All companies expect to increase their *involvement* in the region. However, the form of the involvement—whether additional distributors and sales representatives or joint ventures—is unclear.

9. Iran is considered to be the *primary market* for additional selling and investment efforts in the next five years, followed by, in descending order of priority, Saudi Arabia and Egypt.

10. Iran is expected to *invest in the U.S.* for safety and not control over the company in which investments are made. Additionally, Iran is likely to seek collaboration with U.S. companies for investments in third countries. The objectives of the Arab countries for investing in the U.S. are viewed as being essentially similar to those of Iran.

80

11. With respect to *investments in Asia,* Iran is expected to place almost as much weight on political as on economic considerations. The Arab countries are expected to follow a pattern similar to Iran's except that they are likely to place greater weight on religious considerations.

12. Companies expect to *assist* Iran in undertaking foreign investments by identifying specific projects, by adopting the initiative in presenting proposals to the Middle Eastern countries, and by developing appropriate personnel and organizational structures and orientations. The approach for the Arab countries is expected to be essentially the same as for Iran except that companies will have to be more specific in their proposals.

In reviewing the expectations of U.S. companies regarding the foreign investment climate in Iran, Egypt, and Saudi Arabia at present and in five years, the fundamental theme which emerges is one of change and uncertainty: The foreign investment environment will change and the organization and orientation of the company will also change. Therefore, the IC must attempt to anticipate and plan for change and uncertainty in planning business development in the Middle East.

SECTION 2: INVESTMENT LIFE CYCLE

The IC possesses a wide range of resources such as technology, management, organization, capital, and access to international markets. In undertaking an investment in a particular country,

81

the IC offers different combinations of one or more of these resources. The terms of investment are negotiated between the IC
and the host government, especially in developing countries, at
the time of entry by the IC. The negotiations include questions
such as the nature and type of technology, extent of ownership,
capitalization structure including the extent of foreign exchange
component, management control, extent and type of local employ-
ment effect, extent of exports, training of host-country nationals, and commencement of production by designated time periods.

The act of negotiation and agreement means that the host
government assigns a value to the resources introduced by the IC.
The IC in turn assigns a value to gaining access to resources
available in the host country such as raw materials, cheap labor,
end markets, local capital, and host-country good will.

The values assigned by the host government to the resources
introduced by the IC in a particular investment change with time.
The host country absorbs the know-how and discovers the avail-
ability of alternative sources of supply of similar resources
(perhaps on more attractive terms). Domestic political and economic considerations require changing interpretations (often
negative) of the resources introduced. Thus, these and other
considerations result in the host country later assigning a relatively lower value to the resource contributions initially made
by the IC to a particular investment.

The value assigned by the IC to continued access to host-
country resources also changes with time. The terms of operations
change, generally toward greater restrictions on the enterprise;

82

corporate priorities change in terms of product and/or geographic focus; the degree of integration of host-country operations with the larger multinational operations changes. These and other considerations cause reassessment of the value of continued access to the resources of each in contrast to the value assigned initially.

Therefore, an essential underlying characteristic of a project is that both the IC and the host country assign *different values over time* to each other's changing value assignments. The decrease in values it assigns to IC contributions results in increasing the negotiation strength of the host government vis-à-vis the IC. Generally, the IC's valuation does not decrease as rapidly as that by the host country. Of course the specific industry, type of project, and its role in overall international operations will have a bearing on the extent of the decrease, if any, of the IC's valuation.

Figure 1 highlights the investment life cycle approach to planning for international business transactions, including the dimension of negotiations. Changes in negotiation strength can be divided into the broad categories presented in Figure 1. Additional stages can be added to the investment life cycle, such as negotiation for expansion of operations. It should be noted that very few projects result in withdrawal from a country.

Figure 2 highlights the general pattern of changing negotiation strength of the IC and host government. Several stages of negotiation exist prior to the entry stage when formal approval of an agreement is given by the host country.

Usefulness of Investment Life Cycle (ILC). Assuming that the basic

83

FIGURE 1

INVESTMENT LIFE CYCLE AND NEGOTIATION STRENGTH

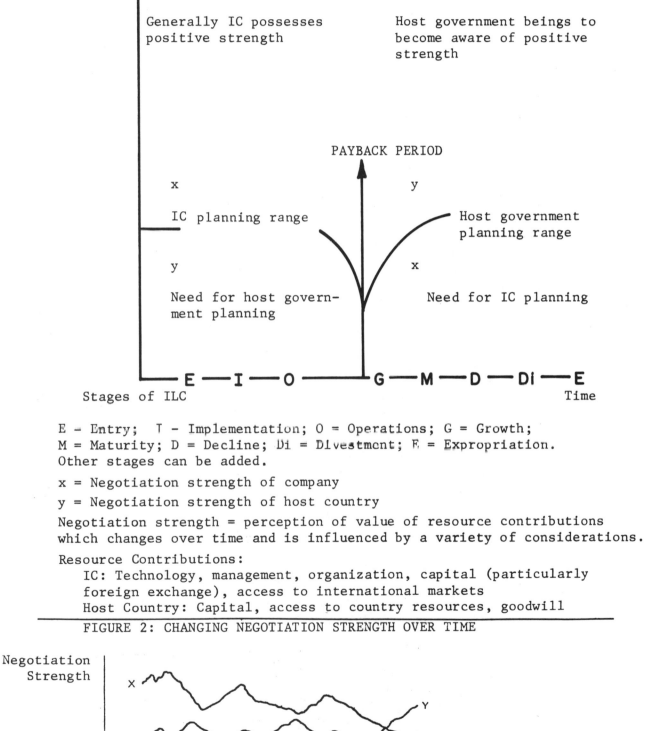

Negotiation Strength

Generally IC possesses
positive strength

Host government beings to
become aware of positive
strength

PAYBACK PERIOD

x   y

IC planning range   Host government
                           planning range

y   x

Need for host govern-   Need for IC planning
ment planning

— E — I — O ———————— G — M — D — Di — E

Stages of ILC   Time

E – Entry; I – Implementation; O = Operations; G = Growth;
M = Maturity; D = Decline; Di = Divestment; E = Expropriation.
Other stages can be added.

x = Negotiation strength of company

y = Negotiation strength of host country

Negotiation strength = perception of value of resource contributions
which changes over time and is influenced by a variety of considerations.

Resource Contributions:
    IC: Technology, management, organization, capital (particularly
    foreign exchange), access to international markets
    Host Country: Capital, access to country resources, goodwill

FIGURE 2: CHANGING NEGOTIATION STRENGTH OVER TIME

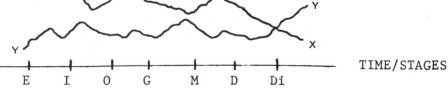

Negotiation
Strength

X

Y

Y

X

TIME/STAGES

E   I   O   G   M   D   Di

idea of changing negotiation strength is recognized by the IC and the host government, six important uses of ILC can be noted:

1. ILC facilitates planning for negotiation with reference to an investment by recognizing the reasons and the implications for changing negotiation strength, which are generally in favor of the host country. Acceptance of this characteristic by the IC would ease recognition of the fact that the contractual and ownership rights of the IC will be honored by the host government only as long as it feels that in balance the country is gaining. ILC is also useful for the host government. It demonstrates that the government is not more powerful than the IC at all times and is especially weak during the early stages of a project.

2. ILC encourages the IC and the host country to emphasize their relative contributions to each other's objectives over time.

3. ILC encourages decision makers and planners to evaluate resource contributions as they influence negotiations, directly or indirectly. Negotiation is an activity and process that is used to give expression to the relative weights assigned by the participants to the respective resource contributions. This outlook requires a more focused approach to the evaluation and use of contributions than one which limits itself to blanket statements such as "social responsibility" and "contributions to host-country goals."

4. ILC can be used by the IC at the country, regional, and headquarter levels for internal planning and communication regarding the relative strength of a project in a particular country.

5. ILC assists in simplification of a highly complex, subjective, and changing range of variables that affect the process and outcome of negotiation over time.

6. ILC stresses the need for visualizing and planning for an investment over its life cycle. The IC, therefore, must plan for an investment by going beyond the point of a payback period.

There are several areas not covered by ILC:

1. It cannot specify the exact shape of the negotiation strength curve except to state that over time, in a specific investment, the strength of the IC is likely to decline, whereas that of the host country is likely to increase.

2. It cannot specify the pace of movement of the negotiation strength curve through different stages of ILC except that the pace appears to be accelerating.

3. It cannot specify the length or duration of a stage of ILC except to observe that increasingly each stage is being reduced in time.

4. It is based on the judgment (subjective expectations) of decision makers in both the IC and the host country.

5. It is not predictive in the specific sense of saying what will happen, when, why, and how. But ILC is predictive in the more general sense of highlighting the broad changes in negotiation strength over time.

The basic uses of ILC are: to assist an individual and an organization to develop a wider and longer perspective, to recog-

nize the changing power relationships, and to anticipate, plan, and effectively implement specific actions which are expressed through negotiation.

ILC and the New Middle East. Figure 3 highlights some stages of negotiation occurring prior to securing approval by the host government of a formal agreement for entry.

The vast majority of proposals by U. S. and other foreign companies are at the pre-entry stage. A few have proceeded to the stage of entry and implementation while a mere handful are at the operating stage. Therefore, the foreign company must recognize that, at the initial stage of negotiations for entry, any project it undertakes will proceed through the balance of stages of the ILC and the consequent changes in negotiation strength of the company and the host country. Planning for the project should recognize the changes likely to occur and the possible stance of the host country and the company to such changes.

SECTION 3: MAJOR STRATEGIC PLANNING CONSIDERATIONS

The strategic planning considerations discussed in this section are host-country associate/partner, expatriate personnel, developing host-country nationals, government relations, multinational competition, multiplier effect, and negotiation.

Host-Country Associate/Partner. Host countries are placing greater weight on using nationals as distributors/representatives and as partners in joint ventures. Therefore, a fundamental question of

87

FIGURE 3

STAGES OF NEGOTIATION

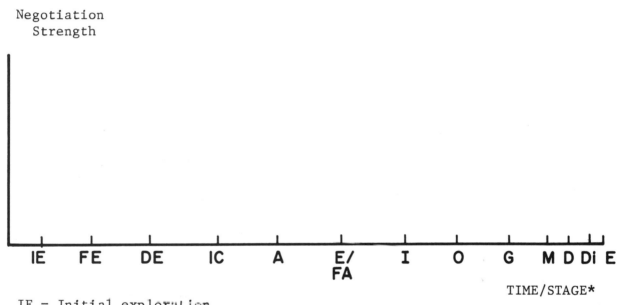

Negotiation
Strength

IE   FE   DE   IC   A   E/   I   O   G   M D Di E
                                     FA

TIME/STAGE*

    IE = Initial exploration
    FE = Field exploration in host country
    DE = Detailed exploration reflecting continued interest
    IC = Initial commitment in principle by company and/or by host country
    A = Reaching agreement between parties
E/FA = Formal approval of agreement by host government leading to entry
  I-O-G-M-D-Di-E = same as in Figure 1

*The stages can be modified depending upon the specific characteristics
of a project.

critical importance for the IC is how to cultivate effective and lasting relations with the host-country associate/partner.

Several issues of a strategic planning nature need to be recognized. First, as the pace of exports in terms of range of products and services and volume grows, the IC will face a growing need for locating distributors and representatives. However, the type of skills required of the local representative will reflect changes over the life cycle. At the initial stages of pre-entry negotiation, the local representative is likely to be particularly important in terms of contacts with appropriate host-country private and public organizations in order to secure an order or to promote a particular venture. An understanding of the local context and contacts becomes the primary input.

As the involvement proceeds into implementation and operations, additional functions are required of the local representative. These include greater technical and managerial sophistication and inter- action with the IC on a growing range of issues. Therefore, an im- portant planning consideration for the IC as it selects a local representatives is to recognize that the IC will need to devote par- ticular attention to the training of the local representative.

The second planning consideration which is closely related to the first one is that in many cases the local representative/distri- butor will become the local partner of the IC in a joint venture. In this context, the local partner has a far more intimate relation- ship with the local operations and development plans of the IC.

The IC will be faced with the particular challenge of securing the constructive participation of the local partner. The vast

majority of local partners have a "trader" mentality which is not
necessarily consistent with an outlook required for industrial
operations. The IC will have to cope with this dichotomy especially as a project proceeds beyond the pre-entry stages into
implementation and operations.

Again, the IC will have to assign particular importance to
the training of the local partner. However, this task will not
be easy because of the sense of power of the local partner, his
limited industrial background, and his conviction that money can
be made in the short term. Additionally, the limited experience
of the expatriate in the Middle East will add to the complexity
of training.

The IC will need to devote particular attention to effective relations with the local partner--especially when the local
partner is the host government. The sensitivities and considerations of nationalism, along with limited willingness and experience
(especially by ICs from the U.S.) in dealing with host governments,
will make this a particularly challenging area. The IC will need
to be particularly skilled as it proceeds beyond the entry stage.

Three significant areas of conflict with the local partner
are likely to emerge as companies proceed to the post-entry stages.

1. Both the IC and the local partner will experience an
    expectation/reality gap; what each party expected of
    the other in terms of inputs and performance will be
    different from what is achieved in reality.

2. The foregoing experience is likely to encourage a
    review and reassessment of the mutual expectations

of the IC and the local partner. The local partner will not be willing to accept responsibility for non-performance by the joint venture and will assign the blame to the IC. This scenario is likely to be true, particularly in arrangements where the host government is a local partner.

3. The foregoing scenario (under 2. above) is likely to raise three alternative courses pertaining to the nature of the role of the local partner: (i) There will be greater involvement of the local partner to ensure that the IC makes the promised contributions; in this situation the local partner adopts a watchdog role. (ii) The inadequacy of the local partner to effectively contribute to the management of the enterprise will be recognized by the host government. Therefore, greater overall management control of the project will be relegated to the IC. In this context, the local partner will become a silent investor seeking financial returns and options to participate in additional ventures undertaken by the IC in the host country and perhaps elsewhere. (iii) The foregoing scenario (under ii above) is what actually occurs; however, because of nationalistic and other image considerations, the local partner is given the proper titles but only limited responsibility.

As to which one of these scenarios predominates will depend upon the nature of the project, the expertise of the foreign company, the attitude of host-government officials and the local

partner, and the relationship between the expatriate personnel and the host-country partner.

Upon reaching an agreement for entry, the IC should embark on an action program for effective participation by the host-country partner. The following areas are illustrative of the types of programs the IC will need to consider:

1. The IC's experience in other developing countries is likely to be useful in structuring effective relationships with the local partner in the Middle East. Therefore, appropriate inputs should be made, especially from the developing Asian countries, because of their relatively greater similarity with the Middle East in terms of socio-cultural factors. The organizational structure within the IC will require modifications to permit the consideration of experience from Asia and elsewhere.

2. The chief executive officer (CEO) in the project must have the skills to deal effectively with the partner. Additionally, the CEO must recognize that a central objective of his assignment is to train and develop the local partner, while keeping in mind the changing requirements of the project over time.

3. The IC must prepare itself for the conflicts which will arise with the local partner as projects proceed to implementation and beyond.

4. The IC should develop a list of other projects it might undertake in the host country to serve as a source of leverage in dealing with the local partner and the host government.

Expatriate Personnel. U.S. and other ICs have demonstrated a
phenomenal growth of interest and involvement in the new Middle
East, and in the coming five years the IC will be involved in a
larger range of projects than it is at the present time. This
dramatic escalation, however, is occurring without the presence
of executives with meaningful experience in the Middle East and
will pose many problems for the IC.

The expatriate managerial cadre being assigned to the Middle
East often have no Middle Eastern experience and in some cases no
international experience. Yet, the operating context of the new
Middle East will impose severe tests on these managers.

For example, the Middle East is a non-Western environment.
The concept of work, social relationships, role of government, and
ways of thinking are significantly different from Western patterns.
(The Asian context, however, reveals greater similarities to the
Middle East.) The expatriate manager will not only be faced with
the task of educating himself about the nature of the environment
but at the same time will be attempting to educate host-country
nationals. This will be a formidable task.

Additionally, the expatriate manager is very often likely to
be uncertain of his own commitment to the country. Moreover, he
will probably reflect upon whether a Middle Eastern assignment is
a desirable step in his career progression. The absence of old
"Middle East hands" at senior management levels will not contribute
to a growing Middle Eastern orientation and/or understanding at top
management levels. Therefore, when the expatriate manager is first
assigned to the new Middle East the key questions he is likely to

93

pose to himself and the organization are: What is the long-range commitment of the organization to the region? How will my career development be influenced?

Severe demands will be made on the expatriates' family life. The lack of educational, recreational, and cultural facilities-- along with the severe restrictions on the role of women--will take its toll in terms of unhappy families, making for unhappy executives.

The task of the expatriate technician is not likely to be any simpler. He will be faced with the additional task of trans- ferring know-how to host-country nationals about whom he knows very little and who in turn have very limited if any industrial background. At the same time, the technician will be faced with additional hurdles in the transfer of know-how to host-country nationals caused by the sociological and psychological dimensions of sudden wealth--an attitude which says "Why should we get our hands dirty if we can buy it?"

The IC has not fully recognized the significance of these issues largely because most projects are at the entry or pre-entry stages. However, it is safe to state that the real test of the expatriate will begin as a project enters the stages of implemen- tation and operations.

The main policy implication for the IC is that it should plan for a failure rate of expatriate executives in the Middle East which is greater than is true in other developing countries. This might require far more training efforts before assigning the executive to the Middle East. Or, the IC might consider sending

94

some of its executives with Asian experience to the Middle East; while such an executive would still require training, such training would not be as extensive as for an executive with no Asian experience.

Additionally, the IC will need to review the duration of assignment of an executive. On the one hand, the socio-cultural context of the Middle East and the strong role of personal relations might encourage a longer duration of assignment than is normally the case in other countries. Conversely, professional and family considerations might call for a faster rotation policy.

Expatriate technical personnel, who will be responsible for implementation, should be complemented by non-technical personnel with an understanding of the socio-cultural context of the host country. In this way, the problems of transfer of know-how can be reduced.

Developing Host-Country Nationals. The IC will be faced with the task of rapidly training nationals in managerial and technical positions along with recruiting and training a work force. The limited experience of the expatriate and the rapid pace of indigenization sought by host countries will make this a difficult task. The IC will fully perceive the magnitude of this problem as it proceeds into the implementation stage.

Development of a supervisory cadre is an immediate task. Expatriates are neither qualified nor available, or they are far too expensive for such a role. The Arab countries of the Gulf are importing supervisory cadres from other Arab countries,

notably Egyptians and Palestinians. Iran is also beginning to import cadres from Pakistan and other countries. However, the basic objective of the host countries is to seek development of their own nationals. Therefore, when using even Arabs in supervisory positions during implementation, the IC would be well advised to recruit and develop host-country nationals as eventual replacements.

For middle-management talent, in addition to seeking host-country nationals in the U.S. and Western Europe, companies should extend their efforts to include key Middle Eastern universities such as the American University of Beirut and the American University in Cairo, which include students from many Middle Eastern countries. These students establish relationships with their colleagues from other countries in the region and in time might offer a source of regional management talent. Additionally, their professors often have moved to important governmental positions in a line or advisory capacity; former students might gain preferential access to them. Individuals from these sources might well serve the critical function of being the interpreters and intermediaries between the Western expatriate assigned to the Middle Eastern country and the host-country workers and decision-making elites. Of course, such a function will become critically important as projects proceed beyond the entry stage into implementation and operations.

Companies in a particular industry or on a cross-industry basis might explore the support or assistance of one or more host governments in establishing training institutions. Such institutions

would serve to offer specialized programs to host-country nationals in areas of particular shortage in the host country. Foreign companies would provide training material and instructors, and would send their employees for training.

In seeking managerial and technical talent, the foreign company is likely to discover that the public-sector enterprises of the host government house a significant percentage of the local talent. Companies might be tempted to raid such enterprises for their own needs. However, such a move is likely to be fraught with risks of attracting host-government ill will. Additionally, public-sector employees are not likely to possess the orientation toward business operations stressed by the private companies.

Government Relations. The single most important determinant in the longevity of the IC in a host Middle Eastern country is effective relations with the host government. The government serves as the major source of funds as well as the leading organizer and planner of economic activity and industrialization, and decides upon the terms and conditions of foreign investments. An IC functioning in the Middle East therefore becomes strongly and intimately involved with the host government.

At the *pre-entry stage*, the IC has selective interactions with the host government. The local partner plays a major role in introductions for the foreign company and in threading through the maze of local social and procedural requirements. The primary objective of the foreign company is to negotiate the terms of entry; this

involves interaction with a select range of officials in some ministries (generally at the relatively senior levels), especially in the case of large-scale projects. Through the host partner, the objective is to determine who can assist the company in gaining approval of the proposed project, a process which extends over several months if not longer.

At the *post-entry stages* of implementation, the nature and requirements of government relations undergo a change. The permissions provided by the foreign-investment "approving arm" of the host government might not find ready acceptance by other agencies or ministries concerned with interpretation and implementation of the terms. Relatively lower levels of government officials become involved in implementation of the project through actions such as stamping the appropriate documents, issuance of labor permits, and a host of other procedural requirements. Often officials at these levels do not possess the experience or the sense of urgency which the foreign company might have discovered at the relatively senior levels of the government.

Other changes also occur. Given the rapid pace of growth of the role of government in economic planning and industrialization, new agencies and ministries come into being and responsibilities for given industries may shift. This may result in another review by the host government of the original terms of investment with resultant consequences for implementation.

Often the negotiators originally deputized by the company to negotiate entry for the project are withdrawn and the responsibility for implementation transferred to people with a technical background, but who do not understand the art of establishing effective relationships

98

with the host government. This adds to the problems of an already
complex situation.

Within the ministries the power relationships among individuals
might change. This is significant in the context of societies where
the orientation of the decision maker carries a strong weight in the
interpretation of policies or agreements.

In brief, at the post-entry stage of implementation the IC will
experience the need for constant interaction with the host government. The local partner can assist in many of the areas. Yet, the
executives of a project will have to develop their own skills and
resources for interacting with the host government.

The chief executive officer assigned to the project will have
to recognize the absolute need for cultivating effective relationships with the host government. And he will need to develop the
skills and orientation for this task. The wrong attitude on his
part will have a seriously adverse effect on the longevity of the
project and the company in the country. Additionally, while the
company will depend heavily on the local partner it will be important for the company not to place all of its eggs in one basket.
The local partner's influence with the host government is a double-
edged sword: It can help the foreign company but it can hurt it as
well. In order to be informed of the informal relationships and
the shifting power centers within ministries which most affect its
activities, the company will need to structure and develop a system
for gaining access to information. Expatriate Arabs and especially
host-country nationals from well-placed families can play a useful
role in this function.

99

<u>Multinational Competition.</u> The rich Middle Eastern markets are attracting growing interest by private and public enterprises from various parts of the world in sales, turnkey operations, direct investments, and barter arrangements. A wide range of official, semi-official, and private discussions by businessmen and U.S. and other foreign government representatives to the Middle East underscore the awareness of the area's economic potential.

Within the framework of multinational competition, each source of sales/investment will reflect the particular approach of the investing country. For example, the Soviet Union and Eastern European countries are likely to place greater stress on barter arrangements. Japanese companies with their trading background, and as a means of gaining an edge on competitors from Western Europe and the U.S., will also place relatively greater stress on barter arrangements in formulating the overall package of terms for doing business in the Middle East.

The home governments of the selling/investing countries will play an active role because of the importance they attach to the Middle East. Bilateral trade and loan and investment agreements between a Middle Eastern and a foreign country will provide the broader framework for specific projects.

Given the growing importance of the public sector in the Middle East, it is likely that host governments will prefer to enter into arrangements with public-sector enterprises in other countries. The private foreign company will face this additional dimension of competition.

Host Middle Eastern countries will seek diversification of

sources of investment in order to reduce dependence upon any one source. This will add to the overall competitive atmosphere in the region.

At this early stage, competition has been largely for entry--how a company gains approval of an investment or sale in a Middle Eastern country. In light of the high expectation mood toward the region, competition has been keen, as companies vie for entry. However, the issues will change as companies proceed to the implementation and operations stages. Instead of heavy focus on expectation, at the post-entry stages the focus will be far more on fulfillment of expectations, such as actual delivery, training of personnel, and anticipating and catering to the changing interpretation of needs on the part of host-government officials.

The implications for the IC of multinational competition include the following:

1. Recognizing the changing nature of competition over the course of the ILC.

2. Activating different sources of supply/investment available to the IC depending upon which source (e.g., European or U.S.) is likely to be in a better position in the Middle East.

3. Recognizing that terms of selling/investment by a company will be exposed to multinational competition.

Multiplier Effect. Host Middle Eastern countries possess a limited industrial base and are seeking a broad range and rapid pace of industrial development. The IC will play an important role in these development efforts both within the host countries and also in

101

collaborating with host countries for projects in third countries.
At this stage, the vast majority of projects are at the entry or
pre-entry stages. It is safe to assume that, before long, host
countries will seek additional projects by foreign companies in a
growing range of local industries which they wish to develop. Foreign participation will be sought and it is not unlikely that companies which are favorably known to the host country will probably
have a better chance of participation in the additional projects
than those which are not well positioned. Conversely, an unfavorable performance by a company in an initial venture will have a
seriously adverse effect on opportunities which might subsequently
arise in the host country.

It is important, therefore, that at the initial stages of gaining
entry into a host country the IC attempt to *identify additional
projects* which it might wish to undertake in the host country and
through collaboration in third countries. In this way, it can
demonstrate a sense of long-range commitment to the host country
which can serve as a means of negotiation strength in dealing with
the host government and the local partner and also assure expatriate
employees of the company's continuing involvement and interest in
the region.

Negotiation. Negotiation is the use of common sense under pressure
to achieve objectives. It consists of four "Cs": *C*ommon interests
to have something to negotiate for, *C*onflicting interests to have
something to negotiate about, *C*ompromise on terms and conditions,
and *C*riteria/objectives of the negotiation. In the context of

102

change and uncertainty in the Middle East, it is safe to assume
that there will be a fresh interpretation of the four Cs by the
host countries (government and local partner) and the foreign
company. These changes will require re-negotiation of the original terms of entry achieved by the foreign company.

More specifically, other considerations are likely to prompt
re-negotiation of the original terms of entry. Both foreign companies and host countries have entered into projects without a
full awareness of what can and cannot be achieved or how long it
will take to achieve project targets. The lack of precedents
has added to the overall uncertainty of target dates and stages
of project fulfillment. However, commitments have been sought
and given. When the project proceeds into the stages of implementation and operations, it is likely that the original target
dates and stages will not be fulfilled, thus encouraging re-
negotiation of the original terms.

Host Middle Eastern countries are gaining additional experience
in development planning and dealing with the IC. In time, they
are likely to seek modification of terms of participation by the
foreign company on issues such as ownership levels, royalty rates,
and pace and adequacy of training nationals.

Alternative sources of investments will bolster the negotiation strength of the host countries. Therefore, companies
entering the Middle East are in the nature of first-generation
investors who have been granted certain investment terms. Eventually, the host countries will seek additional investors. Certain
investors such as Japanese companies might be more willing to offer

change and uncertainty in the Middle East, it is safe to assume that there will be a fresh interpretation of the four Cs by the host countries (government and local partner) and the foreign company. These changes will require re-negotiation of the original terms of entry achieved by the foreign company.

More specifically, other considerations are likely to prompt re-negotiation of the original terms of entry. Both foreign companies and host countries have entered into projects without a full awareness of what can and cannot be achieved or how long it will take to achieve project targets. The lack of precedents has added to the overall uncertainty of target dates and stages of project fulfillment. However, commitments have been sought and given. When the project proceeds into the stages of implementation and operations, it is likely that the original target dates and stages will not be fulfilled, thus encouraging re-negotiation of the original terms.

Host Middle Eastern countries are gaining additional experience in development planning and dealing with the IC. In time, they are likely to seek modification of terms of participation by the foreign company on issues such as ownership levels, royalty rates, and pace and adequacy of training nationals.

Alternative sources of investments will bolster the negotiation strength of the host countries. Therefore, companies entering the Middle East are in the nature of first-generation investors who have been granted certain investment terms. Eventually, the host countries will seek additional investors. Certain investors such as Japanese companies might be more willing to offer

relatively more attractive terms because of their desire to penetrate the host country. The host country would view the original terms as the most favorable and seek to negotiate terms relatively more favorable for the host country. Within this context, the original investor will be faced with re-negotiation of the original terms of entry.

The IC must plan for the re-negotiation of its original terms of investment—not only from a legal standpoint but from the standpoint of changing resource contributions. The ILC outlined in Figure 1 offers one approach. Additionally, the IC should adopt two specific moves to be effectively positioned for re-negotiations. First, one of the executives involved in negotiations for entry should remain involved in the subsequent implementation of the project. Many understandings and a feel of the situation are developed during the course of a negotiation which are best understood by the negotiators. The continuous presence of a negotiator in the project will assist the company in reducing some of the conflicts which might arise otherwise. Second, the chief executive officer of the project should be alerted to the fact of re-negotiation so that his job description adopts a wider outlook than one of merely project implementation.

CONCLUSIONS

The Middle East is an attractive market but it is not an easy one to develop on a long-term basis. A long-range commitment will have to be made at the most senior levels of management if the IC wishes to have a continuing and profitable presence in the region.

The test of foreign projects will begin as more companies move into the implementation and operations stages. The foreign company

104

will learn immensely in terms of what can and cannot be achieved and what are realistic expectations of doing business in the Middle East. On their side, host governments will develop a sharper understanding of the requirements of industrialization in terms of resources required (in addition to money) to nurture long-range development. In short, both the host countries and the IC will be going through an educational process about each other and about themselves.

Appendix A

MAJOR MISTAKES IN NEGOTIATION

Developing a list of "do's" and "don'ts" in negotiation is always
fraught with dangers of simplification and oversight. However,
the following list illustrates types of mistakes commonly committed
by the multinational corporation (MNC) in negotiations with host
governments in developing countries, including the Middle East.

Failure to place yourself in the other person's shoes: It
is not sufficient merely to know the position and approach of your
opponent to a negotiation; even more important is to understand
the reasons which prompt him to adopt the particular stance.

Insufficient understanding of different ways of thinking:
Reaching the same conclusions is important, but in negotiations
it is even more important to know the thought processes by which
individuals from different cultures reach the same conclusions.

Insufficient attention to saving face of the opponent:
"Winning" in a negotiation situation should not result in a loss
of face for the opponent, especially in countries where personal
honor is a sensitive issue.

Insufficient knowledge of host country: Often the negotiator does not have sufficient knowledge of the history, culture,
and political characteristics of a country in which he is negotiating.

*Insufficient attention to problems of communication because
of language difficulties:* Misunderstandings often arise because

the negotiating parties do not know each other's mother tongue or because they underestimate differences of meaning and inter-pretation even when the mother tongue of one of the negotiating parties is used.

Insufficient recognition of the nature and characteristic of the role of government in centrally planned economies: The desire for rapid development, the distrust of private enterprise, and the lack of indigenous entrepreneurial talent have prompted host governments to play a major role in planning for the economic development of their countries.

Insufficient recognition of the relatively low status assigned to businessmen: Not only are government officials in planned economies powerful, but they often look down upon the businessman who is viewed as being concerned only with questions of profits and not the broader national aspirations of the society.

Insufficient recognition of the role of host government in negotiations: Negotiations in developing countries are generally tripartite in nature--involving the foreign company, the local company, and the host government.

Insufficient recognition of the perception of host countries of the role of the MNC's home government in negotiations: Regardless of what the reality of the situation is, the host government believes that the foreign company uses the muscle of its home government in negotiations with the host government.

Insufficient recognition of the economic and political criteria in decision making: Host government officials place particular stress on political considerations in evaluating investment propo-

sals in keeping with the general orientation of the type of organization to which they belong.

Insufficient recognition of the shifting value of precedents: Each negotiating party seeks to establish precedents or gain an interpretation of existing precedents which are favorable to it.

Insufficient recognition of the difference between approval at one level and implementation of such approval at other levels of the government: Gaining approval of the central government for an investment does not mean that other levels of the government will automatically implement the approval.

Insufficient understanding of the role of personal relations and personalities in decision making by the host government: Host government officials possess considerable discretion in interpretation of policies and regulations relating to foreign investments.

Insufficient attention to implications of removing all negotiators as the project progresses from negotiations for entry to implementation: The understandings and personal relations established during negotiations are critical in the subsequent interpretation of the formal agreement. More often than not, while the company engages in a complete turnover of personnel upon gaining approval of agreement for entry, the host government continues to involve one or more of the negotiators.

Insufficient recognition of the informal process of negotiation: Typically, meaningful progress in negotiation is made through the informal process which requires allocation of adequate time and an understanding of the socio-cultural characteristics of the host country.

Insufficient allocation of time for negotiations: It simply takes longer in certain countries to present a proposal, to gain a reaction, and to offer a response because of distance, mutual suspicion, different ways of thinking, and the internal decision-making structure of the government and the MNC.

Insufficient attention to planning for changing negotiation strength: The negotiation strength of the IC and the host country changes over the duration of a project.

Interference by headquarters: Headquarters personnel sometimes interfere directly in negotiations causing serious damage to the credibility of the country-level managers and the field negotiations.

Insufficient planning for internal communication and decisions: Several parts of an organization have an interest in an ongoing negotiation and their views and preferences have to be recognized in negotiating for a particular package of terms of investment.

Insufficient recognition of the role of the negotiator in accommodating the conflicting interests of his group with those of the opposing groups: The negotiator plays a crucial role as interpreter, intermediary, and counselor both to his own group and to the opposing group on what can be achieved in a particular negotiation.

Insufficient recognition of the loci of decision-making authority: Decisions are seldom made by any one branch of government but are shared across agencies and ministries because of the particular characteristics of government organizations.

109

Insufficient recognition of the strength of competitors:
The tendency to underestimate the competitive strength and
negotiation skills of non-U.S. companies is a source of weak-
ness in the U.S. company's planning for negotiation.

*Insufficient attention to training executives in the art
of negotiation:* Executives are seldom trained or encouraged to
develop negotiating skills.

APPENDIX B

OBVIOUS BUT OFTEN OVERLOOKED CHARACTERISTICS

OF DOING BUSINESS IN THE MIDDLE EAST

The following list is for purposes of illustration and is relevant for many developing countries:

1. Generalization: Avoid generalizing too much about the region because there are significant differences between, and also within, individual countries.

2. Time: In the U.S., time is like an arrow shot through space which does not return to a point it once crosses. In the Middle East, time is like a wheel which returns to the same point time and time again.

3. Individuality: In the Middle East (unlike the U.S.) the individual is viewed within the context of a group to which he belongs. Aggressiveness and self aggrandizement by an individual are disapproved.

4. Generation gap: The younger generation (under 25 years of age) in the Middle East possesses an outlook and orientation toward life and development that differs from that of the previous generation.

5. Form of expression: In the Middle East the subtle and oblique manner is used instead of the direct and blunt approach.

6. Relationships: Meaningful relationships are formed only over a period of time and not through a few encounters.

7. The total person: The Middle Easterner prefers doing business with a person whom he knows personally. Therefore, there is limited differentiation between the personal and professional side of a relationship.

8. Maturity: In the Middle East, it is believed that knowledge and maturity come with experience and experience comes with age.

9. Evaluation: The basis of evaluation of a person and the time span used is different from that in the U.S.

10. Forget stereotyped images: Do not view a Middle Easterner in the context of a stereotyped image.

11. Appearance: The American simply looks different from a Middle Easterner.

12. Going native: Don't try to be too Middle Eastern, because you simply cannot.

13. Tip of the iceberg: Demonstration of a western way of life (dancing, etc.) are often for the convenience of the westerner. Look beyond the surface and you will find a far more traditional outlook on life.

14. Role of government: The government is the central point of reference for the Middle Eastern businessman.

15. Difference between approval and implementation: Getting approval from a government does not mean that your problems are over. In fact, they might be beginning as you attempt to implement the approvals.

16. Decision making: Decisions by a government are the result of deliberations among a wide range of officials in a number of ministries and agencies. Therefore, decisions take time.

17. Economic and political: What is largely an economic issue for an enterprise is often largely a political issue for the host government.

18. Communication chasm: Unlike corporate executives, the career background of host-government officials seldom includes experience in business and economics, and this results in a different orientation to problems and their solutions.

19. Power of bureaucrats: Do not offend the bureaucrats; they are powerful. Remember the saying: "Ministers may come and ministers may go but bureaucrats stay forever."

20. Thinking process: In the Middle East, as important as solving a problem is the manner in which it is solved.

21. Colonialism: The vast majority of Middle Eastern countries have experienced colonialism by people mostly from unrelated cultural and racial groups. And for many Middle Eastern countries, political independence was achieved only recently.

22. Don't moralize about business, personal, and political ethics: Recognize the overall system of life in the Middle East and remember that everybody has some skeletons.

23. <u>Remember you are a guest</u>: The rules of behavior for a guest should be recognized.

24. <u>Know your host country</u>: Everybody feels his country is important.

25. <u>Equality</u>: Middle Easterners demand to be treated as equals, particularly by westerners. Nationalism is a major force prompting actions by Middle Eastern countries to achieve this objective.

Bibliography

Books

Business Prospects in the Middle East: Opportunities for Financing, Trade and Investments. New York: Business International, 1975.

Hitti, Philip K. *Islam: A Way of Life*. Chicago: Henry Regnery Company, 1970.

Kapoor, Ashok. *Planning for International Business Negotiations*. Cambridge, Mass.: Ballinger Publishers, 1975.

Lenczowski, George (ed.). *Political Elites in the Middle East*. Washington, D.C.: American Enterprise Institute for Public Policy Research, 1975.

Mansfield, Peter. *The Middle East: A Political and Economic Survey*. New York: Oxford University Press, 1973.

Periodicals

"Algeria: A New Twist to Selling Knowhow," *Business Week*, April 14, 1975.

"All about the New Oil Money," *Newsweek*, February 10, 1975.

"Arab and Iranian Students Increasing at U.S. Colleges," *New York Times*, March 28, 1975.

"Arab Emphasis on Aid," *Financial Times* (London), No. 26,627, March 27, 1975.

"Arab Telecommunications Survey," *Financial Times* (London), No. 26,594, February 17, 1975.

"Arabs in Western Europe: Unseen but Not Unsensed Economic Force," *New York Times*. March 30, 1975.

"Aramco is Taking a New and Direct Role in the Industrialization of Saudi Arabia," *Wall Street Journal*, March 20, 1975.

"As I See It: A Talk with Iranian Minister Hushang Ansary," *Forbes*, Vol. 115:7, April 1, 1975.

114

Bill, James A., "The Plasticity of Informal Politics: The Case of Iran," *Middle East Journal*, Vol. 29: 2, Spring, 1973.

Bowring, Phillip, "A Long Wait For Asia," *Far East Economic Review*, Vol. 85:32, August 16, 1975.

Carey, Jane P., "Industrial Growth and development Planning in Iran," *Middle East Journal*, Vol. 29:1, Winter, 1975.

Chenery, Hollis B., "Restructuring the World Economic Structure," *Foreign Affairs*, Vol. 53:2, January, 1975.

Demaree, Allan T., "Arab Wealth as Seen Through Arab Eyes," *Fortune*, Vol. LXXXIX:4, April, 1974.

"Group May Bid for Saudi Deal," *Financial Times* (London), No. 26,562, January 10, 1975.

"Growing Presence in the Middle East--Japanese Banking and Finance VIII," *Financial Times* (London), No. 26,543, December 16, 1974.

Hitti, Said H., and Abed, George T., "The Economy and Finances of Saudi Arabia," *IMF Staff Papers*, Vol.XXI:2, July, 1974.

"How Kuwait is Spending its Surplus," *Financial Times* (London), Vol. 26,458, October 7, 1974.

"I'm the Shah, Fly Me," *The Economist*, Vol. 254:6861, February 22, 1975.

"Iran Again Buys a Share of Big German Concern," *New York Times*, April 10, 1975.

"Iran Faces Difficulties Placing Surplus Funds," *Financial Times* (London), Vol. 26,472, October 24, 1974.

"Iran-Pan Am Deal Endorsed by U.S.," *New York Times*, February 16, 1975.

"Iran Stake in Euro-nuclear Plant," *Financial Times* (London), Vol. 26,556, January 3, 1975.

"Iran to Buy British Stake in German Babcock and Wilcox," *Financial Times* (London), Vol. 26,637, April 14, 1975.

"Iran Will Spend $15 Billion in U.S. Over Five Years," *New York Times*, March 5, 1975.

"Iranian Economy: The High-flying Magic Carpet," *Financial Times* (London), Vol. 26,486, October 10, 1974.

"Iran's Plans Revised," *Middle East Economic Digest*, Vol. 18:38, October 20, 1974.

"Iran's Race for Riches," *Newsweek*, Vol. LXXXV:112, March 24, 1975.

"Japan Borrows $100 M. From Saudi Arabia," *Financial Times* (London), Vol. 26,467, October 18, 1974.

Kaji, Mottoo, Richard Cooper, and Claudio Segre, "Towards a Renovated World Monetary System," *The Trilateral Commission*, Triangle Papers No. 1, Tokyo, 1973.

Karmanfarmaian, Khodadad, et. al., "How Can the World Afford OPEC Oil?," *Foreign Affairs*, Vol. 53:2, January, 1975.

Kraar, Louis, "The Shah Drives to Build a New Persian Empire," *Fortune*, Vol. LXXXX:4, October, 1974.

"Krupp Signs Iran Deal," *Financial Times* (London), Vol. 26,467, October 18, 1974.

"Kuwaitis' Big Stake in Lonhro," *Financial Times* (London), Vol. 25,521, November 20, 1974.

"Lonhro has Arab Slice of Costain," *Financial Times* (London), Vol. 26,610, March 7, 1975.

"Lonhro Ltd. Says Arab Investors To Buy Big Stake," *Wall Street Journal*, March 7, 1975.

"Lonhro Says Investors From Kuwait Will Buy 11% Stake in Concern," *Wall Street Journal*, February 19, 1975.

Mancke, Richard B., "The Future of OPEC," *Journal of Business* (University of Chicago), Vol. 48; 1, January, 1975.

"Middle East: Now Foreign Workers Rush to the Oil Lands," *Business Week*, March 17, 1975.

"Middle East Survey," *Banker*, Vol. 125:589, March, 1975.

Moorsteen, Richard, "OPEC Can Wait--We can't," *Foreign Policy*, Vol. 18, Spring, 1975.

"Muslim States Favored in OPEC Aid Programs," *Financial Times* (London), Vol. 26,612, March 10, 1975.

"OPEC Petrodollar Surplus Could End by 1980," *Financial Times* (London), Vol. 26,578, January 29, 1975.

"OPEC, The Trilateral World and the Developing Countries: New Arrangements for Cooperation, 1976-1980," *The Trilateral Commission*, Triangle Papers, No. 7, New York, 1975.

"Petro-Aid Takes Off," *Economist*, Vol. 254:6860, February 15, 1975.

"Pipeline From Iran," *Time*, Vol. 705:16, April 21, 1975.

"Prospects for Krupp in Iran Joint Venture," *Financial Times* (London), Vol. 26,619, March 18, 1975.

"Rich Markets in the Middle East and a World Rush to Cash In," *U.S. News and World Report*, Vol. LXXVIII, No. 11, March 17, 1975.

Rustow, Dankwort A., "Who Won the Yom Kippur Wars," *Foreign Policy*, Vol. 17, Winter 1974-75.

"Saudi Arabia Favors Private Economic Initiatives," *Middle East Economic Digest*, Vol. 19:13, March 28, 1975.

"Saudi Arabia Keeps a Tight Hold On its Purse Strings," *Financial Times* (London), Vol. 26,532, December 3, 1974.

"Saudi Arabia Lacks Enough Openings for Expenditure," *Middle East Economic Digest*, Vol. 18:33, August 16, 1974.

Schmidt, Helmut, "The Struggle for World Product," *Foreign Affairs*, Vol. 52:3, April, 1974.

Walter J. Levy, "World Oil Cooperation, or International Chaos," *Foreign Affairs*, Vol. 52:4, July, 1974.

Stauffer, Richard V., "Middle East: Potentials and Problems," *The Conference Board Record*, February, 1975.

"Syria, A Special Report--Development Plan," *Financial Times* (London), Vol. 26,612, March 11, 1975.

"The Middle Eastern Stake at Daimler-Benz," *Financial Times* (London), Vol. 26,530, November 30, 1974.

"The New Arab Ideas on Money," *Financial Times* (London), Vol. 26,632, April 4, 1975.

"The Saudis Look to the Future," *Wall Street Journal*, March 28, 1975.

"The Year Arabia Discovered Money and Europe Discovered Arabia (And Iran)," *Economist*, Vol. 254:6855, January 11, 1975.

"$26,000 Million to Flow into Algerian Economy," *Middle East Economic Digest*, Vol. 18:35, March 1, 1975.

"U.S. Hopes for Iranian Hospital Contracts," *Financial Times* (London), Vol. 26,603, February 27, 1975.

"U.S. in $15 Billion Deal with Iran," *Financial Times* (London), Vol. 26,608, March 5, 1975.

Welles, Chris, "The Battle for the Petrodollars," *Institutional Investor*, Vol. VIII, No. 11, November, 1974.

"What Oil Sheiks Cannot Buy," *Financial Times* (London), Vol. 26, 573, August 27, 1974.

"Why Bates Wants to Go Arab," *Financial Times* (London), Vol. 26, 583, February 6, 1975.

"Why Iran Wants to Save Pan American," *Business Week*, March 3, 1975.

United Nations' Reports

"Demographic Characteristics of Youth in the Arab Countries of the Middle East. Present Situation and Growth Prospects, 1970-1990," *Studies on Selected Development Problems in Various Countries in the Middle East, 1968*, United Nations Economic and Social Office in Beirut, 1968.

"Financing of Industrial Development in the Various Countries of the Middle East," *Studies on Development Problems in Selected Countries of the Middle East, 1973*, United Nations Economic and Social Office in Beirut, 1974.

"Growth and Development Perspective in Saudi Arabia," *Studies on Selected Development Problems in Various Countries in the Middle East, 1968*, United Nations Economic and Social Office in Beirut, 1968.

"Regional Plan of Action for the Application of Science and Technology to Development in the Middle East," United Nations Economic and Social Office in Beirut, 1974.

"Some Aspects and Problems of Foreign Private Investment in the Middle East," *Studies on Development Problems in Selected Countries of the Middle East, 1973*, United Nations Economic and Social Office in Beirut, 1973.

"Some Aspects of the Development of Human Resources in Various Countries of the Middle East," *Studies on Selected Developmental Problems in Various Countries of the Middle East, 1968*, United Nations Economic and Social Office in Beirut, 1968.

"Some Social Aspects of Industrialization in Selected Countries of the Middle East," *Studies on Selected Development Problems in Various Countries in the Middle East, 1968*, United Nations Economic and Social Office in Beirut, 1968.

NOTES